WHAT OTHERS

IR

"Both inspirational and calming, energ... ...elaxing, *Steady Days* provides realistic tips that challenge mothers without making us feel overwhelmed. I loved reading this book; the concepts make so much sense! From small steps to creating a daily routine, to encouragement to become a more contagious mother, Jamie Martin has crafted a stellar handbook for moms in need of affirmation."

—Tsh Oxenreider, writer and editor of the popular blog SimpleMom.net and founder of SimpleLivingMedia.com

"We're all busy. We all wish we had more time to spend with our children. And we wish the time spent with our children was less harried, more meaningful, and more playful. *Steady Days* helps you achieve those goals. Read this wonderful book—it's worth it, for you and your children!"

— Jennifer Trainer Thompson, author of *The Joy of Family Traditions: A Season-by-Season Companion to 400 Celebrations and Activities*

"Jamie Martin has mapped out an honest and personal approach to managing the complexities of modern family life. Her thoughtful and understanding manner will have parents and caregivers alike wanting to learn more about her ideas for building a steady and loving family."

— Rae Grant, author of *Crafting Fun: 101 Things to Make and Do with Kids* and *Cooking Fun: 121 Simple Recipes to Make with Kids*

"After reading this book I have walked away with not only many tools to create a smoother day for my children, but more importantly a greater sense of purpose for my days. Jamie Martin gives insight into the 'bigger picture' of time spent with young children and she has empowered me to mother intentionally, rather than dragging through the day wondering what to do next."

— Jill T., mother of three and early childhood educator

"*Steady Days* challenges in a way that makes the reader feel empowered, not incompetent."

— **Caroline R., mother of two, teacher, and writer**

"I so badly wish someone had handed me *Steady Days* before I brought my first child home from the hospital. It should be 'standard issue' for new moms, especially those used to being professionals."

— **Robyn P., mother of nine, entrepreneur, and founder of ViveVita**

"Jamie Martin is much of the reason and inspiration for what I feel I am able to accomplish each day. She helped me think about 'professionalizing' my home life just like I did my life in the corporate world. I feel I've become more intentional at home with my children because of her example, and I have enjoyed time with my kids even more because of her great ideas."

—**Tara R., mother of two and founder of The Momentum Group**

"*Steady Days* is well-written, clear, and useful to 'transform mothering, one family at a time.' Can I have a do over with my kids?"

— **Jill M., mother of three grown children and president of Strategies for Living Unlimited**

Steady Days

A Journey Toward Intentional,
Professional Motherhood

Jamie C. Martin

Infused
Communications

Infused Communications
P.O. Box 4668 #34640
New York, NY 10163-4668
www.infusedpublishing.com

© 2009 by Jamie C. Martin

9 8 7 6 5 4 3 2 1

First Edition
Printed in the United States of America

Design and Illustrations by Krista Abbott
Photographs by Desirea Rodgers

PUBLISHER'S CATALOGING-IN-PUBLICATION DATA

Martin, Jamie C.
Steady days : a journey toward intentional,
professional motherhood / Jamie C. Martin. -- 1st ed.
p. cm.
Includes bibliographical references and index.
LCCN 2009936151
ISBN-13: 9780984124602
ISBN-10: 0984124608

1. Child rearing. 2. Parenting. 3. Parent and
child. 4. Motherhood. I. Title.

HQ769.M37 2009   649'.1
QBI09-600185

Trishna, Jonathan, Elijah:

You guys are going to change the world.

You've already changed mine.

With a full and overflowing heart,
I give my thanks and love.

Contents

Acknowledgments

Few people are as blessed to have as many cheerleaders as I've had while writing this book. Words fail to adequately convey my thanks, but what follows is my meager attempt.

I must begin with the person who, apart from myself, has spent the most time and energy making *Steady Days* what it is—my friend, editor, and an inspiring professional mama, Caroline Starr Rose. Thank you for grammar advice, many pep talks when my spirit was sagging, and sharing your gifted writing talent with me.

Thanks to Jill M., whose crazy and wonderful dream gave me the courage to begin the whole project, and to the rest of my *Steady Days* ladies: Robyn, Jill T., and Tara—for reading drafts, giving feedback, and staying positive. I'd also like to send a thanks out to Beth, Rebecca, and Annmarie for many helpful suggestions.

I want to thank Krista Abbott for her amazing cover design, layout, and illustration work. Thanks to Desirea Rodgers for photos so good they make me want to be *me*, and for spending quite a few mornings hanging with the energetic Martin Three.

Thanks to my NC family—you always seem to think I can do what I say I'm going to do. Thanks for believing.

Thank you, Sarah, for loving my little people almost as much as I do, and for being part of our family.

I'd like to thank Susan Fitzgerald for putting beneficial editing touches on the final manuscript.

Many thanks to the readers of my blog, www.SteadyMom.com, who have welcomed my little words into your homes. Also to the authors of Mommy blogs everywhere: I feel privileged to share the blogosphere with thousands of creative and hardworking ladies.

Steve, I feel blessed beyond description to live out this adventure called life with you. It doesn't get any better than this. I thank God for giving me the family of my dreams.

To friends and partners of Love146: This thank you is written with continued hope that all children will one day get what they deserve—a safe home. Abolition and Restoration.

Introduction

I am not a perfect mother. Often I struggle with impatience; sometimes I lack the enthusiasm I long for. I make many mistakes, just like my children. As they are maturing as children, I am maturing as a mother. In any career, experience allows us to grow, improve, and learn. But unlike other professions, many of us mothers have never had any training to prepare us for this new job filled with diapers, tantrums, and sleepless nights. We need to equip ourselves with practical tools that allow us to give our personal best to our young children, helping us thrive in our strengths and overcome our weaknesses. We aim for professionalism in every other area of our lives; why should our children get anything less?

My husband and I welcomed three children into our family in less than three years: our biological son, Jonathan; our son Elijah, adopted from Liberia; and our daughter, Trishna, adopted from India. Less than two years separates all three from oldest to youngest. With little experience I found myself trying to care for three young children. My desperation kept me searching for and learning from those with more expertise. Each time I've found a resource particularly helpful, I've altered it to suit our family and have integrated it into our lifestyle. Over the years, I've found that our home life has become more peaceful and manageable.

Steady Days is divided into forty readings presented in short, digestible chapters. Often parenting books contain so much content that they leave readers feeling overwhelmed. To avoid that problem, I've broken this information down into manageable entries—just one or two quick ideas to consider throughout your day. Professional mothers are busy mothers; we need to maximize our resources to get the biggest return on investment in every area, even our reading. Take your time and work through the material at your own pace, fast or slow. Make it work for you.

Use this guide for inspiration and ideas to give your young children what they deserve and crave: you, at your best. These tools can lead to a more peaceful atmosphere in your home for the people who matter most to you. Imagine the ocean: Sometimes the waves pound the shore, and sometimes they roll gently in and out. But within it all there is a rhythm, a consistency, a steadiness. This is what *Steady Days* is all about. We desire that consistency in our homes in spite of life's ups and downs. We create Steady Days for our children by getting organized, retaining our enthusiasm, learning together, and making memories. When we balance these qualities together, we discover the gentle rhythm we long for.

These ideas have enriched my life and family, but you can easily adapt them to suit your unique situation. Choose one or all, whatever will benefit you in the most important profession you'll ever have.

Part One: Getting Organized

The secret of all victory lies in the organization of the non-obvious.
—Marcus Aurelius

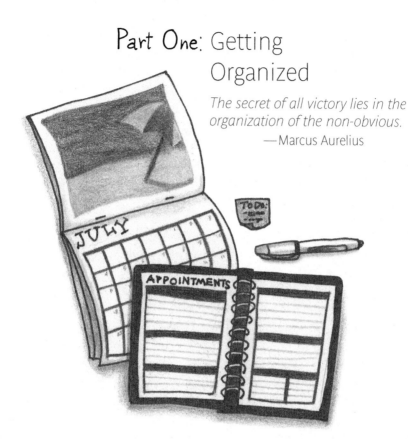

1. What's Your Motivation?

We're moms; we have busy schedules and lots of papers. Bills, receipts, a full appointment book—you name it. Every mother has to come up with a strategy to manage paper clutter and plan her days. A functioning system benefits everyone, including our children.

If, as a mom, I am often struggling to find an important item, missing appointments because I've forgotten them, or just generally disorganized, this creates tension in my household. All of us know that our children quickly pick up on our stress and attitude, even when it is unspoken.

Just this morning I was frustrated with the behavior of one of my sons, Jonathan, but thought I was doing a pretty good job of concealing my feelings. He glanced up at me, and his whole countenance changed. "Mommy," he said, "Are you happy?" I tried to assure him that I was and asked him why he had asked. "Because your face looks a little sad, like this." I wish I could adequately describe the troubled look he mirrored to me at that moment.

Yet again I was struck by how perceptive my children are; nothing slips by them. This is my motivation to stay organized. It's hard to be cheerful when you're running late, for example. Disorganization leads to rushing, which leads to impatience.

I'm often surprised by my behavior toward my children when I'm rushed compared to when I have plenty of time. If I'm feeling pressured, I am less gentle, less attentive, and less pleasant to be around.

Organization is a priority for me because it blesses my children. Even without considering the benefits of productivity or efficiency, the stability of my children depends on my organization. This alone should be my motivating factor.

We live in a society that values organization. Thriving in the "real world" depends on arriving at work on time, achieving realistic deadlines, and managing time wisely. If I want to set my children up for success, I need to take steps to develop these qualities within them, even at a young age. In order to do this, I must ensure these characteristics are well developed in my own life.

A prepared mother looks like a professional. No one would show up at the office for a busy day in her pajamas. And yet there's a stereotype of mothers, particularly stay-at-home mothers, consisting of bathrobes and slippers until 11:00, combined with talk shows and soap operas all afternoon. No wonder motherhood isn't valued in Western cultures. Our jobs as mothers have more long-lasting impact, even on future generations, than almost any business meeting could. By doing my job with intention, I help others redefine what motherhood can and should be.

If I'm an organized woman, I'm able to do more. In this age when there is much to do and many roles to juggle, this is a valuable asset. Who wouldn't wish to add more time to her day? This is the outcome when you have a flexible plan—your productivity and efficiency increase.

It's easy to crawl into bed at night, after the children are finally asleep, and wonder, "What have I accomplished today?" By being intentional with your time, you can actually answer that question and ensure that the answer is what you want it to be. This is another wonderful reason to get organized.

2. | If You're Not Organized, Why Not?

Some people seem to be naturally organized, while others struggle with it. Why is this? If you're not organized, why not? It's not enough to say, "Well, this is just the way I am." We owe it to ourselves and to our children to question everything, asking, "Why do I do what I do?" If the answer isn't one we find satisfactory, we can implement small changes.

Some find that their disorganization is based on years of bad habits. They've had a tendency to lose things, which has continued all their life. Maybe someone has even commented, "You are always losing things!" This further cemented the habit and the mentality that it must be "just the way I am."

Or perhaps their families were marked by disorganization when they were growing up. Disorganized habits might have been modeled for them all their life and they think that this is the way things are done (or not done).

Some people think that if they become organized, they will lose their spontaneity and passion for living. Because they really value these qualities, they think they must accept their disorganization in order to maintain their free spirit. This doesn't have to be the case. Having a flexible structure helps you enjoy spontaneity. If you have taken time to be organized in the things that matter most, then you will not feel behind. So when an opportunity comes your way, like the first warm day of spring or a special concert for the children, you can ditch the rest of your plans and go for it. You can enjoy without guilt, because your other responsibilities are up to date.

Sometimes there may be a deeper reason behind someone's disorganization, or even behind someone's organization. Organization usually comes naturally to me. This has made my life easier in some ways, and more difficult in others. The challenges have been caused by the fact that my original motivation for staying organized was to feel in control of my life and circumstances. While this in itself is not necessarily bad, in my case it often meant that if I didn't have this sense of control I felt frustrated. It also led to a tendency to control others. For a mother, this is an unacceptable motivation for being organized. All of us can remember, as both children and adults, what it feels like to be around a controlling person. This isn't what I want my children to remember about growing up with me as their mother. So I need to seek out the positive aspects of organization and release these negative tendencies. This is a slow but steady process.

Marilyn Paul, a successful management consultant, confronts the issue of organization in her book, *It's Hard to Make a Difference When You Can't Find Your Keys*. She states, "Organization is deeper and more powerful than I once thought. It's not only about freeing ourselves from clutter or putting 'everything in its place.' It's about expanding our sense of personal efficacy. It's also about discovering courage and dignity, and living our true life purpose."[1]

It's easy to think of surface-level problems and results when discussing organization. But the roots go much deeper. As Marilyn Paul describes, piles of papers and other types of disorganization drain us mentally and emotionally. This leaves less of us fully available to our children. Maintaining this panoramic view of organization will help us find the energy to take necessary steps toward change.

3. One Step Toward Organization

It's easy to feel overwhelmed when taking a step toward organization, particularly if you are introducing new habits. My first suggestion is to spend time contemplating the previous chapters, deciding why you want to become organized and what it will do for you when you get there.

I also advise selecting one item at a time to work on. Trying to tackle every disorganized element in your life at once is a recipe for burnout and disaster. Ask yourself, "What one area would improve my life and my children's lives if it had more order?" Start there.

My friend Jackie answered this question by saying that she really wanted a food plan for her children. She felt that because she wasn't organized in this area, her children weren't eating as healthily as she would like. In this case, her motivation was the health and nutrition of her children— something we all believe is important. And that's the key—whatever you try to change must be of such value to you that you will want to continue forward, even in the midst of challenges.

Look for simple first-step solutions. Don't attempt to go from no meal plan to Martha Stewart in a week. If you do, you're setting yourself up for failure. For Jackie, the first step could be as simple as buying some frozen vegetables and microwaving one type each day. The solution doesn't need to be complex to be effective.

Other first steps you might want to tackle could include training yourself to consult your calendar or PDA every morning to avoid forgetting appointments. It could be immediately putting unneeded items in the recycling when you open the mail. Finding a system for filing or laundry could be other first steps. Or if you're always running late, setting your clocks ahead to help you arrive on time might be a perfect way to get started.

After you've identified one area you'd like to start with, the next hurdle is carving out time to brainstorm and create a plan to tackle that issue. This is where I struggle. I like to have long blocks of time in which I can work on and completely finish a project. Those of us with young children know that such opportunities rarely occur at this season in our lives. So I have to be content with investing ten, fifteen, or twenty minutes here and there over a period of several days.

This was the case when I developed my first *Steady Routine* (see pg 28). I needed it to help with my two boys, ages two years and eighteen months at the time. But I couldn't spend hours developing it. So I started with one small step—I spent twenty minutes thinking of one outing for each day of the week. After I implemented that with success, I came up with morning play activities for each day. Slowly, over a period of weeks and months, my *Steady Routine* came together. And with it, I was accomplishing more as a mother and feeling more fulfilled.

Once you solve one organizational dilemma, it's easier to move on to the next. Don't be afraid to try something that may not work. At times I've been amazed that the activities for my children I was most unsure about have turned out to be the most successful (this was the case with "room time," described on page 38, about which I was hesitant initially). The most successful professionals aren't afraid to try new ideas, even if they flop. This should be the same for mothers as well.

4. | Don't Be Afraid to Delegate

None of us are superwomen. Having an organized plan doesn't mean achieving perfection or doing it all yourself. Instead, it is about managing the various roles you play in life: mom, employee, cook, caretaker, wife, and many more.

Our family is very blessed by a wonderful friend, Sarah, who helps with the children and house. The children wait at the window to announce her arrival—she has truly become part of our family. Her hard work makes our lives more peaceful, enabling me to focus on and remember the long-term goals for our family life.

There are different seasons in our lives and in the lives of our families. During certain times we might need more help than during others. When our daughter, Trishna, first joined our family from India, we had a four-, three-, and two-year-old. We hired Sarah to come twice a week to help us transition as a family. After a year, life had become more routine. Now Sarah comes only once a week. Seasons evolve and change, and as professional mothers we can respond accordingly.

So don't feel as though you can never ask for help. If finances are tight, maybe you can trade with another mother. Or you can get creative with your time. Like most busy mothers, I typically do some of the tasks that just won't fit into our days at night after the children are asleep. Remember, you are in this profession for the long haul. You cannot hand in your resignation. So you need to come up with a long-term survival strategy that will allow you to give your children your best.

5. Flexibility—The Key

I often remind myself that flexibility is the key to enjoying the early years of life with young children. This is certainly true when contemplating organization as well. Life with little ones is always evolving. Just when you think you have something figured out, the entire game plan changes, the phase passes, and there's something new to tackle. Some new issue presents itself that needs to be carefully considered and managed. Flexibility allows you to address the next issue with confidence.

I'm in the midst of such a situation right now. My three children have begun waking up earlier in the morning. Whether this is because the sun is up earlier, they don't need as much sleep, or they're just trying to torment me is up in the air. We've always taught our children to stay in bed until Mommy or Daddy comes to get them. This enables us to get dressed before they are out of bed, a vital step in the organization of our day. It's difficult to get ready with three preschoolers underfoot.

But I'm not comfortable with leaving them in bed bored for an hour, even if they would comply. I'm also not comfortable with getting up an hour earlier myself so I'm ready for the day before they're awake. I believe the most effective families learn to compromise. So it's not just about what's best for the children, and it's not just about what's best for me. It's about what works for our entire family. It's easy to lose sight of this and allow circumstances to dictate our actions. But that's not the most professional way to live.

So I've spent some time brainstorming. I've decided to wake up fifteen minutes earlier (a satisfactory compromise). I've also bought several used children books, which are now our "special morning books." We use them only at this time of day, so the children look forward to them. When I hear the kids awake in the morning, I say hello and give them a few books to look at while I finish getting ready. This works well for now, but like most issues in motherhood, soon I'll probably need another idea. As long as I am flexible and open, I can find a solution that will work for everyone.

Any important organizational problem can be solved when you approach it like a professional. This applies to challenges in the home as much as it does to those in the office. We are currently building the foundation for our children's future. Many of their habits and behaviors will be set for life by the time they enter school. By creating a flexibly-structured home life, we help ensure our children's tendencies are positive ones. Who could ask for stronger motivation?

6. A *Steady Routine*
(A Tool for Organization)

A *Steady Routine* is a blueprint for your day and your children's day. A successful teacher wouldn't show up to her classroom without a lesson plan. We wouldn't arrive for a busy day in the office without an idea of what we wanted to accomplish. Our lives at home are no different.

A couple of years ago, I noticed that my day with my children quickly turned to chaos if I didn't have a plan. This was especially true when they were babies and toddlers. I became frazzled and less patient with them— I didn't like myself that way. So I began to brainstorm and gather ideas. For some reason I felt that if I wrote my routine down or made it specific, it meant I was controlling or not spontaneous enough. Now, after years of having a *Steady Routine*, I know that it doesn't make me controlling—it makes me a professional. My motive behind it is not to control my children, but to give them my best. I *care* enough to plan ahead; I also know myself well enough to realize that without a plan I drift along, guided only by my feelings in the moment. That's not the most efficient or powerful way to live.

I wanted a framework that would eliminate the multitude of little decisions I need to make every day ("What are we going to do today? What should we play with now? What's for dinner?"). I wanted it to be flexible and not legalistic, a helpful tool I can refer to when and if I need it. I wanted to intentionally plan for the important memories I hope to make before my children get older. I wanted to make sure my children's lives had a balance of what I believe is important (such as time for playing outside and not too much television time). I wanted to allow my children as much freedom and independence as they are mature enough to handle. I wanted others, in my absence, to be able to care for my children as well as I do. My *Steady Routine* has enabled me to achieve these goals.

My children function beautifully within this gentle framework. They thrive on both its boundaries and its freedoms. I've found that whatever becomes part of our routine becomes a habit, so it doesn't typically require discussion or lead to tantrums. Of course there is free time in the routine as well, both for my children and for me.

Your routine can be as open or as structured as you need and want. Some mothers may choose to make a plan just for mornings; others may structure more of their day. Go with whatever fits your personality and works for you. Make it specific to your life—each person's plan will look different. All of us have a routine of some sort, whether or not we realize it. A *Steady Routine* just enables you to be intentional and choose what's important for your life and your children.

7. | Phase One—One Small Step

Thinking of creating a *Steady Routine* for your day?

Here's how to get started.

The Goal of Phase One: Make one small change to help your days flow more smoothly.

Potential Small Steps:

* ★ Add a healthy side dish to the evening meal.
* ★ Consult your calendar each morning.
* ★ Make a to-do list each day of no more than three items.
* ★ Sort your mail immediately as you open it; handle it only once.
* ★ Create a system for filing.
* ★ Put laundry in to wash first thing in the morning.
* ★ Set clocks fifteen minutes ahead to help avoid being late.
* ★ Pack school lunches the night before to make mornings smoother.

What is one organizational need your family currently has? Spend today considering what small step you can immediately take to meet that need.

8. Phase Two—Add a New Routine

The Goal of Phase Two: Develop a morning, afternoon, or evening routine—a few steps to bring order to the most challenging time of your day.

Need some ideas to get started?

Here are two examples:

An Afternoon Routine:
* Children up from naps/rest time
* Snack
* Story time
* Video (clean or prep dinner during this time)
* Play outside

An Evening Routine:
* Dinner
* Dinner clean-up (kids helping)
* Free play
* Baths
* Pajamas on and in bed

Just a few steps can make a big difference. A new routine can bring consistency to a time that once was tumultuous.

9. | Phase Three — A Full Day's Plan

The Goal of Phase Three: For those who need or want more structure in their days, below is a framework to create a flexible plan for your entire day.

Take a look at this sample *Steady Routine* to gather inspiration and ideas. More samples can be found in Appendix C.

SAMPLE *STEADY ROUTINE:*
MOM WORKS FROM HOME PART-TIME

TIME/DURATION	MOM	CHILD 12 months
8:00 AM	Up, feed baby	Wake up, breakfast
	Take shower, get dressed	Exersaucer time
	Dress child, get ready for outing	
	Outing: M—Groceries T—Gym W—Playgroup Th—Gym F—Shopping or library	
	Arrive home, prepare lunch	Lunch
12:00 PM	Lunch, work from home	Nap #1 (2 hrs)
2:00 PM	Child awake, feeding, play with toys together	
	Outside—Take a walk or Inside—Music time	

(30 min)	Work from home	Video
	Make dinner	Playpen time in kitchen
	Make dinner	Highchair, snack
(15 min)	Look at books together	
(15–20 min)	Structured play (toy rotation)	
5:00 PM	Work from home	Nap #2 (1 hr)
6:00 PM	Dinner	Wake up, dinner
	Clean up	In highchair with toys
	Free play with Mom and Dad	
	Clean up or free	Bathtime with Dad, pajamas
	Bedtime routine with child	Feeding, story
9:00 PM	Work or free	Bedtime

10. *Steady Routine* Draft Worksheet

Use this form to pencil in ideas for your own *Steady Routine*. You can also find this resource in Appendix A and at www.steadydays.com.

1. Start by filling in the non-negotiable items, like work time, your child's school time, mealtimes, wake-up time, and so on.

2. Browse through the suggested activity lists on pages 37–42 if you need extra ideas to fill in the remainder of your day.

3. Begin to plug various activities into your blank routine segments. Switch items around until it seems like you have a good fit. You can always change something later if you find an activity or time isn't working. I typically update my routine once a month as something in our day changes, like naptimes or seasons.

4. Slowly begin implementing your *Steady Routine*, tweaking as you go along and as you find it necessary to make alterations.

TIME/ DURATION	MOM			
Morning				

Afternoon				
Evening				

11. | *Steady Routine*—Tips and Thoughts

* Remember that a *Steady Routine* is not about restrictions—it's about freedom! You can include as much downtime or unstructured time as you'd like and structure just the times you feel are most important in your day.

* Some women like knowing the exact time at which an activity will take place. Others prefer a routine that is more open ended, so they don't feel behind if something unexpected happens. I've found, especially as my children get older, that flexibility makes our lives easier. Depending on your preferences, you can either fill in exact times on your *Steady Routine* (e.g., structured play at 9:30) or just use your routine to guide the order of activities and their duration (e.g., structured play comes after breakfast and lasts for twenty minutes). See the sample schedules in Appendix C for further ideas.

* If you work outside the home and have an in-home caregiver for your child, creating a *Steady Routine* means you know exactly what happens while you are away. Your child is still getting what you have decided is best—this gives you a powerful sense of peace while you accomplish your work elsewhere.

* You can have different *Steady Routines* for different days. For example, if you work Tuesdays and Thursdays and your child is in daycare, you could have one routine for those days as well as a slightly different version for Mondays, Wednesdays, and Fridays. (See Sample Routines 2A and 2B on pages 142 and 144.)

* If you have older children, they can help develop their part of the routine, including scheduling both required items (like a homework time) and free times (like time with friends). Their involvement in creating the routine can help win their willingness to try it.

12. Suggested Activities

Sometimes we feel that as mothers we should intuitively know how to interact with our children. But I remember thinking in the early days, "If only I could see what others do!" If you've ever felt that way, here are a few ideas for activities for children eight years and younger.

* **Free Play**—This is a block of time in which children follow their own imagination in playing. It's an important time, especially for children who arrive home from a highly structured day at school. I find that the older my children become, the more free play they're mature enough to enjoy. And since one of my goals for our family is freedom, I love integrating this into our day. During free play the children choose their activities. You may be playing with them or may be working elsewhere while they entertain themselves. Essentially this is an unstructured time and can take place inside or outside.

* **Structured Play**—As children grow they crave independence and the ability to make their own choices. But I've found that having too many choices overwhelms toddlers and preschoolers. So in our house, we have structured-play times as well as free-play times. Structured play is a time when I play along with my children at an activity I have chosen. We rotate through several activities each week so that we actually use all the toys we have, without becoming bored. By scheduling the activities, I don't have to think of something on the spot, although I can always alter the plan if I choose.

    When we're not using the scheduled toy, we store it away. This helps retain the "wow" factor when it is brought out each week; the children are excited about playing with it again. Structured-play times could include Legos/Duplos, Matchbox cars, musical instruments, different types of blocks, dress-up clothes, Mr. Potato Head, stuffed animals, indoor tents and tunnels, and so on.

* **Art**—Even though crafting doesn't come naturally to me, I still want my children to enjoy developing their creativity. The mess bothered

me at first, but over time I've found solutions: a fitted sheet over the dining table and old T-shirts as smocks. Some moms love coming up with special art projects and gathering supplies. I do this on occasion, but for our standard art time I keep in stock a few easy supplies: washable paints, stamps, coloring books, crayons, glue, stickers, and Play-Doh.

* **Baking**—My children *love* baking with me. It's one of those activities I had always wanted to do with them but never got around to until I made it a regular part of our weekly routine. My three all stand on chairs around our kitchen island, with their own separate bowls and spoons. As I put each ingredient in my bowl, I put a little in theirs so they feel like they are making their own (and they don't interfere with the final product). This is also a good pre-math time, as we measure and count out ingredients.

* **Room Time**—During room time a child plays alone with toys or books in his or her own designated area, such as his or her bedroom, crib, rug, or playpen. This time helps children learn to play independently, which is especially important if they have siblings. If you have young children at home, it is also a time when you can accomplish a task that is difficult to do with little ones around (such as computer time, work time, telephone calls, or laundry). Far from seeing this as a punishment, our children look forward to room time and race up the stairs to get to their rooms. We also have special toys just for room time that they can choose from.

   We began room time as "crib time" when our children were infants and toddlers. If you are trying to begin the room-time concept with an older child who is not used to it, I suggest trying it for just a few minutes at a time. Try using a special new toy available only during this time. Gradually extend the duration as the child begins enjoying room time.

* Rice Table—This has become a wonderful winter and rainy day activity in our house. I filled a large, plastic under-the-bed container (ours has wheels on it) with uncooked white rice, and then added some small cups, Matchbox cars, containers, and spoons. We spread out a huge camping tarp on the living room floor and roll the rice table on top of it. As long as no children throw the rice (it hasn't happened yet!), any small spills go onto the tarp, which I then roll up and shake outside when we're finished. This is a fun sensory activity.

13. | More Suggested Activities

* **Video Time**—The television can become a serious problem for children if overused, but it can also be a wonderful tool if programs are chosen wisely. Since I have three young children and I'm not Superwoman, video time enables me to maintain the peace in our home and still accomplish what needs to be done.

Typically our little people watch a little more than one hour of television per day—sometimes more, sometimes less. We prefer to let our children watch DVDs instead of regular television so they are not exposed to advertising. I seek out shows that are twenty to thirty minutes in length, so I can let the children complete one full show without having to turn it off before it's finished. I wouldn't be happy if someone turned off my show halfway through, so I try to grant them the same courtesy.

I've heard mothers comment that their children get upset when it's time to turn a video off. This happens occasionally to us, too, especially if it's a new show or one they really enjoy. But typically, because our children are used to their *Steady Routine*, they handle the transition to the next activity very well. They know what comes next, so it gives them a sense of understanding and security.

* **Rest/Book Time**—As our children outgrow their naptime, they continue having a rest/book time. For us, this means the children each have a special rest area (such as their bed or the couch) where they go with some special books or quiet toys. Sometimes they fall asleep; sometimes they just play quietly. We have found this time has a calming effect on all of us.

* **Story Time**—When I found out I was pregnant with my son Jonathan, one of the first things I did was buy a book about reading to children. For years I had imagined snuggling and having story time with my child! Of course, since he wasn't even born yet I had to wait a while. But that didn't stop me from planning.

We read off and on throughout our day when the children request it, but I want to make sure we have a short block of time designated specifically for that purpose in our *Steady Routine*. During our afternoon story time we read our library books. Sometimes the children play with toys as they listen; sometimes they don't listen! And sometimes I get a glimpse of that dream from years before coming true, as all three gather around, leaning on me, to look at a picture or ask a question. This has become one of my favorite times of the day and theirs, too. Another advantage of a *Steady Routine* is built-in accountability. My children know when story time is suppose to happen and will make sure I don't skip it.

* **Individual Time**—For families with more than one child, individual time is a chance to connect one on one and give each child focused time and attention. There are many different ways to do this. Sometimes my husband and I will split up in the evenings, one of us taking a child upstairs for some special time. During this time the child can pick the activity and enjoy having Mommy or Daddy give him or her undivided attention.

At other times we have assigned each child one night per week for individual time. On their evening, they get to stay up a little later and play with us downstairs.

Currently we have extended our bedtime routine so that each child can have a few quiet moments with each parent individually. This has changed from our earlier days when the goal was merely to get all the children in bed as quickly as possible. Now that our children are a little older and more communicative, we enjoy taking a little time to have a brief talk about the day together. I'm often amazed at the insights and comments that arise from the children during these moments; they make the few extra minutes a worthwhile investment in our relationship.

There are many ways to accomplish the goal of individual time, but the idea is to recognize your child as an individual, not just a member of the corporate body of "children."

* **Transition Time**—Recently I was lamenting the fact that transition times are some of the most chaotic in our household. When it's time to change activities or go somewhere, our peaceful rhythm can go downhill fast.

But a recent idea has revolutionized what was once one of the most trying times of our day. I assigned each of the children a special spot in our living room. They can see and talk to each other, but they are not close enough to touch anyone else. When I tell them it's time for special spots, they take a toy or book and sit down.

I can't completely describe how invaluable this technique has been to me when preparing for outings, gathering supplies for a new activity, or making a short phone call. I can even manage to go to the bathroom alone! Amazing.

Sometimes I ask the children to use only whispers during transition time, which helps to keep things calm while we prepare for what's next.

14.	*Steady Home Planner*
	(A Tool for Organization)

Soon after beginning my career as a mother, I felt frustrated with the number of items I referred to regularly throughout my day: my calendar, to-do list, address book, shopping lists, cookbooks, and more. I wanted everything together in one place where I could quickly access it.

This led to the creation of my *Steady Home Planner*, a binder in which I have inserted what I want and need to help me have Steady Days. My binder stays put in my kitchen so I can refer to it multiple times every day. I like knowing exactly where to find important papers when I need them.

There's nothing fancy about the *Steady Home Planner*. It's a standard binder with dividers inside. Yet I would be ill equipped to handle what life throws my way without it. I would also be less patient with my children if I hadn't found a method that works for me.

You may have a paper-organizing system that you love. If so, great. Mine is not the perfect answer for everyone. But if you're in need of a new method, take a look.

Want to make your own *Steady Home Planner*? These items might help:

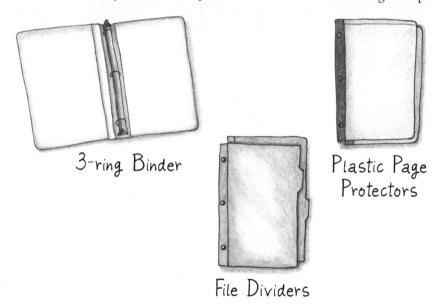

3-ring Binder

Plastic Page Protectors

File Dividers

The first step in compiling your home planner, determining which sections are most important to you and most valuable to your lifestyle, is discussed in the next two chapters.

A Steady Home Planner helps you have smoother, more efficient days.

15. What's Your Motivation?

In this chapter and the next, I give you some ideas of possible *Steady Home Planner* sections. For your own planner, pick the sections that work for you.

Many binders have pockets on the inside cover. This is a good place to keep blank index cards to jot down lists or notes.

Front Section: Use the first section of your binder for the important items you refer to often. In my binder, this includes the following:

* **Emergency Phone Numbers**—The front section of my planner includes a card with important emergency numbers to leave with babysitters.

* **Long-Term To-Do List**—I keep a list of things I need to do in the near future, like scheduling appointments or writing reports. They're not items that need to be done immediately, but I know if I don't write them down, I may forget them.

* **Current Monthly Calendar**—Here I keep track of my appointments and scheduled activities. I like having the entire month in view at one time.

* **My *Steady Routine*—**I keep this in the front section for quick and easy reference throughout the day. I also have a page with our current meal plan and ideas for extra activities I can do with the children.

* **My Weekly To-Do List**—I used to find myself frustrated when I would get to the end of my day only to discover that nothing was accomplished from my daily to-do list. If you have small children, you can probably relate.

    I discovered that a weekly to-do list enables me to stay organized *and* flexible at the same time. I write down specific tasks I hope to accomplish during the week, without specifying the day. I can fit those projects in as my week progresses, without feeling behind. Typically I find I am able to get everything on my list done by the end of the week.

* **Current *Steady Blessings* Page**—See page 62. I keep this page close at hand to make note of the beautiful, and often unexpected, blessings that flow my way throughout the day.

* **Current Important Documents**—At times I will temporarily put in my front section a document that needs immediate attention, like a doctor's form to complete or something I want to keep on hand for a while.

Calendar Section: If you use paper calendars you'll want to have a calendar section in your binder.

* **Future Weeks'/Months' Calendars**—Here I jot down plans for the upcoming weeks and months as they arise.

* **Current Year Calendar**—I find it handy to have the entire year at a glance when I need to plan for an upcoming business trip away or visualize when guests are coming months down the line.

* **Special Date Organizer**—This list helps me keep track of all the important birthdays, anniversaries, and special dates I need to remember. You can find this resource in Appendix A and at www.steadydays.com.

Lists Section

* **Shopping Lists**—You may want to keep multiple copies of your various shopping lists here for easy access. I have three lists: one for the regular grocery store, one for a natural food store, and one for everything else. When it's time to shop, I can grab a list, circle what I need, and go.

* **Menu Planning List**—There are many ways to plan meals. Some people like to plan in advance exactly what they will be having for dinner throughout the upcoming week.

I've tried weekly planning in the past, but found it didn't work for me. I like to plan the *type* of meal I want to make, without specifying exactly which meal it will be. Here's an example:

Monday—Chicken dish
Tuesday—Burgers or pasta
Wednesday— Leftovers
Thursday— Rice dish
Friday—Tortilla dish
Saturday—Leftovers
Sunday—Pizza

I find this balances organization with the flexibility that allows us to use the ingredients and produce we have on hand. I also enjoy knowing in advance which nights I plan on cooking and which nights I don't.

Phone/Address Section

⋆ **Phone/Address Book**—Here's a place for often-used numbers, as well as for those referred to only once in a while, like numbers for work colleagues, church directories, and doctors' offices that you call once a year.

⋆ **Internet Directions**—I developed my *Steady Home Planner* after we'd recently moved to a new area of the country. It seemed I was always looking for directions online. So in this section of my binder I keep copies of directions I may need again in the future. You could also have a quick and easy reference list of addresses to use with your GPS system.

⋆ **Restaurant Menus**—My husband and I got tired of the hassle it can be to find a nighttime babysitter, so we recently began having date nights at home. Once a week we order takeout after the children are in bed, eat at the dining table with candles and music, have adult conversation, and perhaps watch a movie.

We still go out sometimes, but the difference is we are intentional about our nights in, as well, and I enjoy it just as much if not more than a night out. So in this binder section I keep copies of the takeout menus we use most often.

Meals/Cooking Section

⋆ **Recipes**—I got tired of stopping in the middle of preparing dinner to go look something up in a cookbook. To avoid this interruption, I made copies of the twenty recipes I use most often, put them in page protectors, and inserted them into my Home Planner. This saves me from running to different cookbooks every night; I always have what I need on hand.

⋆ **Cooking Chart**—I also copied a fresh-vegetable cooking chart from one of my cookbooks that tells me how to cook every vegetable you could imagine. It saves me a lot of trouble when I'm trying to figure out how long to steam the Brussels sprouts.

Back of *Steady Home Planner*: Here you can insert some sturdy plastic folder pockets to hold items of nonstandard sizes like postcards, bank slips, doctor's notes, or stamps. I also keep information I know I will need again in the future, like our Christmas dinner menu and other special holiday lists.

Other Potential Sections: I created my Home Planner to help me achieve Steady Days. You should do the same. Make it as similar to or as different from mine as you need it to be. Other ideas for sections include the following:

* **Work Plans/Projects/Ideas**—Maybe you need to have on hand forms from the office or just a central place to jot ideas as they come to you throughout the day.

* **School Papers for Children**—Report cards, field trip slips, homework assignments, yearly school calendars—keep it all together!

* *Steady Blessings* **Section**—It says a lot when gratitude is so important that it even fills our Home Planners.

* *Mom's Favorite Moments*—See page 106. Quickly and easily write down those memories you don't want to forget!

* **Children's Goals**—You may want a section to remind yourself of chores you want to teach your kids, self-help skills to work on, or things that need to be accomplished before a vacation or field trip occurs (like books to read or projects to complete).

17. Questions & Answers—Getting Organized

1. Does every mother need a *Steady Routine*?

Every mother functions best when she's being intentional with her time and energy. How this plays out practically will look different for everyone. For some it will be very structured, and for others less so. But in either case a well-thought-out plan will result in the best for our children.

A stay-at-home mother with one child may function efficiently with a much less formal routine in place. But those of us who have multiple children, work outside the home, or juggle other roles may need a more structured plan to maximize our time and efficiency. There are also likely to be certain seasons in our lives when we need more structure, and other seasons when we need less. A *Steady Routine* helps you accomplish what otherwise might not be achieved.

2. I have a new baby. Naptimes are irregular and I am up in the night for feedings. How can I possibly be organized?

Life transitions like a new baby can throw the best plans out the window. Whenever a new child has joined our family, I have always scaled back significantly on nonessentials like cleaning and extensive meal preparation. My goals at such times are to keep up with dishes and laundry, and there are even days when that is unrealistic.

Of course it's impossible to create a timed plan when you don't know at what hour your baby will be eating or sleeping. But if you feel you need a gentle order to your day, you could make up a bare-bones *Steady Routine* without any times. Instead you could list the order in which you want to do a few activities. Then, depending on when your baby is eating and sleeping on a given day, you can hop around on the schedule and know what you need to do during that time. (And make sure your own rest is an important priority during a new baby's naptimes.)

Another idea helped me when my two sons were thirteen months and six months old. This was a challenging time in many ways. I couldn't implement a detailed routine with much success. I was in survival mode, but I was frustrated by the feeling that I wasn't accomplishing much. So I made a long list, in two columns, of all the potential activities I might need or want to do with the boys or in the house (play activities were also included). I printed it and put it in my *Steady Home Planner* in a page protector. Then, as I went through my day, I used a dry-erase marker to cross off the activities we did. This served two purposes: It helped me see that I was accomplishing something during my days, and it also gave me ideas if I needed to fill time with an activity. I used this for several months until the season of our life changed and I could implement a routine with a bit more structure.

3. I keep finding myself falling behind on the routine, and I can't seem to catch up. What can I do?

It depends what you mean by "falling behind." Remember, you made the routine to work for you; you don't work for it. So you can't really fall behind what you created. Circumstances change all the time with young children; the unexpected arises and a professional mother has to deal with it. When this happens, the key is not to panic. Your routine is exactly what can help you in these moments. I recommend looking at your plan and switching activities around so that what is most important gets accomplished. The rest can wait.

I am at a stage where I know our routine well enough that I don't often have to refer to it on paper; typically things flow fairly well, and I can look at it if and when I need an idea. It provides a level of stability for us, but it isn't something to make me feel as though I am behind in any way.

Part Two: Retaining Enthusiasm

Reflect on your present blessings,
of which every man has many;
not on your past misfortunes,
of which all men have some.
—Charles Dickens

18. A Converted, Contagious Mother

An important aspect of being an intentional mother is loving what you do and translating that love to others. Whatever your career choice, enthusiasm can make you a professional. I was reminded of this recently by one of the workers who picks up our garbage every Tuesday. Carl is my three-year-old son's hero, and he always puts a smile on my face as well. Every week as he passes by our house, he looks up at our window, where at least one, if not all three, of my children stand in awe, watching. He raises his hand in a celebrity-style wave, a smile gleaming on his face. We feel encouraged as he continues on his way. True professionals inspire others.

Enthusiasm is contagious, so surround yourself with others who are passionate about their life's work. Enthusiastic friends motivate and encourage us to continue on our chosen path, even in the midst of daily challenges.

I'm convinced that children also want to be around this positive type of influence. If we don't love what we do as mothers, our children notice quickly. Our attitudes, positive or negative, influence them in a matter of minutes. How can we convey our love for them? By choosing to enjoy the daily tasks we perform, embracing the moments that will never be back again. We can stop what we're doing when they need attention, letting them know how important they are.

It's easy, both in motherhood and in our other careers, to begin with high hopes, yet quickly become discouraged. I've found, through my own experience and talking with other mothers, that the most continually effective moms have gone through what I call a "motherhood conversion" experience.

I can remember the first Thanksgiving after the birth of my son. We had been invited over to a friend's house for a traditional dinner. When we arrived, my two-month-old was asleep in his car seat. I had heard that you should let your baby learn to sleep through noises, so even though my host offered to let me put Jonathan in a separate room, I said I was sure he'd be okay out in the main area. Guess who was awake less than ten minutes later? From that moment on, I was completely distracted by my little bundle of neediness. Just when I sat down to eat, he cried. Throughout the night, I had to stop what I was doing and never got to finish a conversation, and by the end of the evening I felt a little resentful. Driving home that night, I thought, "Wow. I'm not going to be able to do what I want anymore." Multiply that by the three amazing children I now have, and you can imagine this type of situation occurs frequently in my life.

The other shocking fact, which I knew before having children (but you never *really* understand until you live it), is the idea that there are no holidays from mothering. Growing up with the traditional school year filled with holidays and long summer breaks or working in jobs with vacation time and sick days doesn't prepare parents for this completely consuming role. Even if you work outside the home, at the end of your "work day," you are transitioning to another job. It's a beautiful job—don't get me wrong—but downtime is generally a thing of the past.

These are some of the things that surprised me about motherhood. Gradually, however, I began to welcome the dynamics of my new life. I decided to try and embrace them as wholeheartedly as possible, instead of fighting inner battles over the interruptions to "my" time. This was my conversion experience. Once I was able to accept the fullness of my new life, it then became possible to enjoy it much more.

This is a daily process and a daily choice. Every time I reach a new phase in my career as a mom, I discover the need for a new conversion experience. Such was the case a few weeks ago when my middle child stopped needing his afternoon nap. I struggled so much with this transition. My children's naptime is one of the few quiet parts of my day, when I actually have time to do what I choose and still be productive before everyone wakes up. The idea of drastically shortening this time did not come easily to me. But when I stopped thinking selfishly, I was able to look for creative solutions. In this situation, creativity involved brainstorming methods to keep my son entertained while still allowing some downtime for myself. We're still working on this transition, but I find myself feeling more positive. These moments of conversion help me maintain my enthusiasm as a professional mom.

Every household experiences difficult days, and there are seasons when positivity just doesn't come naturally. I am far from arriving at the enthusiasm summit I hope to reach, but each day I make the choice to try and embrace what comes. In the following chapters I share some methods I've discovered to keep the joy flowing.

19. | Discipline or Punishment?

Somehow, as I was growing up, I got the idea that good parents don't *ask* children what they want to do; instead, good parents *tell* children what they are going to do. Now I believe this is simply untrue. This authoritarian tendency, which I'm slowly growing out of, comes from a desire to control. If we don't recognize it, the wrong parenting mindset will steal our enthusiasm.

Of course, disciplining our children is an important part of parenting, but it's still only *one* part of parenting. In addition, discipline is not the same as punishment. Positive discipline focuses on the long-term goal of teaching and instilling good habits that will benefit our children. Punishment, on the other hand, focuses on getting back at children for their inconvenient and annoying behavior. It's often accompanied by anger and irritation.

I've done both, and I can vouch from my experience that children know exactly which mindset we have. They mirror in behavior and speech the messages they receive from us. If we enjoy being with them and respect them as unique individuals, then they enjoy being with us and find it easier to respect us. If we approach them with enthusiasm, they're more likely to approach us in the same way. It *is* possible to be a gentle, compassionate, and still effective voice of authority in your home.

Along the same vein, I've found that saying no all day steals the joy from my home. With three lively preschoolers under my roof, it's easy to get to the end of a day and find I've been saying no continuously. Of course, there are some things to which we must say no; that is part of our job as mothers. But what I'm referring to is the tendency to take the "kidness" out of our kids. That beautiful, impulsive, carefree behavior has much to offer us if we slow down enough to appreciate it and don't try to force our children to act like adults.

20. | The Value of Compromise

Another quality that yields enthusiasm to a professional mother is the ability to compromise. Within a home, the routine of life needs to work for everyone in order to bring joy. It's not all about what I need as a parent, and it's not all about what they need as children. We've all seen the two extremes: parents who continue living as though they have no children, as well as households in which the child's every whim is met no matter what. Neither of these extremes results in a positive home.

The home is about a family; it isn't about each individual. So give and take is involved, compromise is required, for the sake of a peaceful atmosphere. It's a delicate balance, but I can tell the special moments when we manage to achieve it. Everyone's needs are being met, and everyone is also giving of themselves and their preferences in order to meet those needs.

One example of compromise in our home involves our morning routine. A few years ago the children had free time to play after breakfast while my husband and I got organized for the day ahead. We called it free time, but it more honestly could have been termed "fighting time." Our children were at an age and stage where they were not capable of being in the same room unsupervised for more than thirty seconds without screams erupting. It was difficult and frustrating for everyone.

So we decided to save playing together for times of the day when I was there to supervise. And in the morning the children play individually at various activities they choose. This has revolutionized our mornings and has been an effective solution for the whole family. I'm able to get things done, and the children are able to play creatively without having to battle over the same toy. We still have occasional issues during this time, but in general this compromise has benefited everyone.

21. Inspiration and a Steady Heart

Gaining fresh inspiration is key to maintaining passion. There are many ways to do this. I love reading biographies of world-changers like Mother Teresa, Martin Luther King, Jr., and William Wilberforce. Their stories remind me of the broader perspective behind my mothering. My daily work is impacting future world-changers. Who could ask for a more worthwhile occupation?

A sense of spirituality also yields inspiration to millions around the world. My personal faith as a Christian shapes every decision I make and guides me on a daily basis. It has completely transformed my life's purpose, and enthusiasm goes hand in hand with a deep sense of significance.

A recent study conducted by the Paris School of Economics and the European Centre for Social Welfare Policy and Research investigated claims that religious individuals are happier than those who aren't religious. After analyzing data from thousands of European households, the researchers found that those with a religious faith reported a much higher level of life satisfaction than nonbelievers, even when faced with a difficult life event like the loss of a job.[2] I have found this to be true in my life as well. Having a living, active faith to pass on to our children is truly a gift in these days when many people fail to find a meaningful purpose later in life.

No matter how many good intentions I have on any given morning, there are some days or weeks that feel far from Steady Days. Steadiness is what I aim for as a professional mother, but you'll find no perfection in my home. There are just some times in our lives that seem unsteady and rocky. Some things are just unpleasant and have to be dealt with.

After returning from India in 2007, having completed our daughter's adoption, everyone in our family ended up with head lice for weeks. We were trying to adjust to a new child, recovering from severe jet lag, and taking care of three preschoolers, all with very itchy heads. As you can imagine, it was the complete opposite of the rhythm I hope for in my home.

And yet, what keeps me going in the midst of unpleasant difficulties is a Steady Heart. This is even more important than a Steady Day, because if you have a Steady Heart, the Steady Days will soon follow. A Steady Heart contains a sense of purpose, the idea that you know *why* you are doing what you're doing, even down to the most mundane of tasks. Everything is involved in the big picture, so everything is important.

A Steady Heart comes from focusing on the end goal of raising our children into amazing individuals of character and influence. A Steady Heart is accompanied by a passion that allows us to follow our intuition, even when it goes against the majority. We can calmly take big risks and try new things, and with such challenges come enthusiasm. Our children are watching. May our Steady Hearts inspire their own, and may our Steady Hearts lead to Steady Days in our home.

22. Steady Blessings
(A Tool for Enthusiasm)

Gratitude is an important contributor to retaining your enthusiasm and even your health. Recent studies completed by the Institute for Research on Unlimited Love found that being grateful increases your body's antibodies, sharpens your mental skills, lowers your blood pressure, and helps limit depression.[3]

In 2003, psychologists Robert Emmons and Michael McCullough came to a similar conclusion in their study entitled "Counting Blessings Versus Burdens: An Experimental Investigation of Gratitude and Subjective Well-Being in Daily Life."[4] Emmons and McCullough sought to discover scientific evidence confirming the often-promoted idea that gratitude can improve one's outlook. Can gratitude actually create a positive perspective, or is it merely a quality those with a naturally positive outlook already have?

The study involved over 400 people. Participants were randomly assigned to record one of three things: their hassles, their neutral life events, or their blessings. The results suggested that writing down and focusing on your daily blessings contributes to an increased sense of optimism, determination, and energy. Those who recorded their blessings were also more likely to help others and less likely to experience depression. They slept better, and even their spouses noticed a positive change in them.

I find that in the midst of the day-to-day with my children, it's easy to get caught up in the little problems and forget the larger perspective. But taking a few minutes to write down blessings and special moments reminds me to seek the joy in the midst of the mundane. It's the little things, like my son saying, "I really love you, Mommy," or a friend's phone call, that provide a boost of encouragement for the day.

Steady Blessings are just that, steady. They are always present in our lives; we need only to stop and look for them. For the good of our health, our enthusiasm, and our children, why wouldn't we?

Want to make your own *Steady Blessings* Book? These items might help:

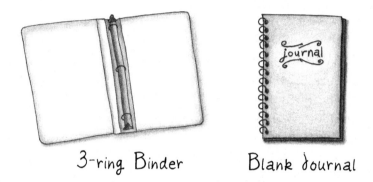

3-ring Binder   Blank Journal

Ideas for different types of *Steady Blessings* Books are given in the next chapter.

23. | Make Your Own *Steady Blessings* Book

There are several ways to integrate *Steady Blessings* into your life. You can find templates for the first three options described here both in Appendix A and at www.steadydays.com.

* **Parent's Version**—This worksheet contains space for several days of entries. They are all undated, so don't feel guilty if you miss a day or even a week. The point of recording your blessings is to add positivity to your life, not to add another obligation that must be fulfilled. Writing down your *Steady Blessings* is totally on your terms. Keep in mind, though, that Emmons and McCullough found that those who recorded their blessings daily received more favorable benefits than those who only recorded them weekly.

* **Mom/Children Combined Version**—This version developed as a way to cultivate the habit of positive thinking with our children. The template has a place at the top for Mom and/or Dad to write their *Steady Blessings* and a space at the bottom for the child to write or draw his or her blessings. I am excited about making this an after-dinner activity with our entire family when the children get a bit older.

* **Children's Version**—This form is specifically designed for children to use on their own. Young children can draw or paint what they're thankful for. This is an easy art time idea. Older children can write their blessings and illustrate them, if desired.

* **Blank Book**—Of course, there's no magic formula for recording *Steady Blessings*. Use the designed templates if they appeal to you, but any scrap of paper will do. Or you can always use a blank journal.

Steady Blessings is an especially valuable tool for moms working outside the home whose children spend part of their day with a nanny or at daycare. Asking your childcare provider to jot down a few positive things your child did or said during the day makes you feel more involved when you're not able to be there.

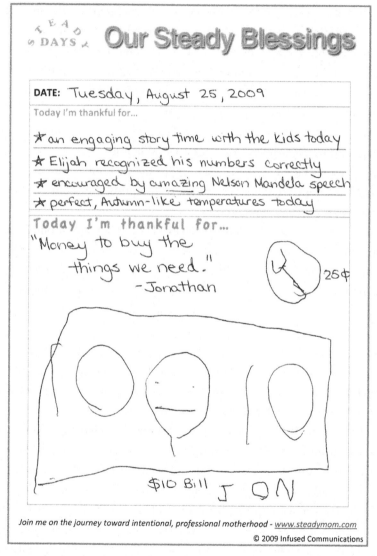

Jonathan and I created this Steady Blessings sheet together.

24. Steady Thought Cards
(A Tool for Enthusiasm)

I believe one of my jobs is to inspire my children. I can do that only if I am inspired myself. Sometimes it's difficult to keep up the inspiration, so I'm always searching for new sources of encouragement. Because of my love for reading, I often come across an incredible thought that impacts me and that I'd like to remember. I used to sometimes jot a quote down in a journal, but then I wouldn't come across it again for months. I wanted to have these great thoughts as a consistent part of my life, inspiring me to continue enthusiastically with my work.

This led me to create *Steady Thought Cards*. They are ideas I can dwell on throughout my day when challenges arise. When my day starts to become hectic, meditating on *Steady Thoughts* helps me remember the big picture. My cards currently include a mixture of Scripture and quotes from key authors, philosophers, and educators.

One of my current favorites is by Henry David Thoreau: "If one advances confidently in the direction of his dreams, and endeavors to live the life which he has imagined, he will meet with a success unexpected in common hours."[5] Keeping such an inspiring thought present throughout the day provides an underlying sense of purpose and focus to my work with my children.

You can use *Steady Thoughts* in a variety of ways. I enjoy flipping to a new card every morning, having one selection to meditate on daily. You may choose to put them up around your house or desk area, or carry them in your car. Find out what works for you.

Words thoughtfully chosen carry the power to challenge and change lives. I want to teach my children the power of words, how to choose them wisely and kindly as they speak. I also want to teach them to meditate on and be influenced by great thoughts. I see *Steady Thought Cards* as an effective way to accomplish this goal. I plan on creating a set for them as well when they're older. I can add selections I want them to meditate on, and they can choose some too. This is a positive way to influence without nagging, helping prepare them for the challenges that may unfold in their day. It also opens the door to deeper conversation with children, providing opportunities to discuss inspiring quotes together.

Now when I come across powerful words, I know exactly where to put them. My collection of *Steady Thought Cards* continues to grow and change. You can see my sample quotes in Appendix A and at www.steadydays.com. Add your own to maintain your inspiration.

Inspired professionals are successful professionals; as professional mothers, may our inspiration overflow to our children.

Want to make your own *Steady Thought Cards?* These items might help:

Index Card Box

Index Cards

Steady Thought Cards provide much-needed daily encouragement.

1. I didn't have a good mothering role model growing up. How can I find one now or get the perspective I need to overcome what I lacked as a child?

If you grew up without a positive mother figure in your life, it's easy to feel lost when you become a mother yourself. But an intentional mother can take the time to analyze what isn't working, knowing that otherwise there will be consequences that continue to be passed down to more children. There are ways to prevent this from happening.

My advice is to consider and even write down the characteristics you do want to emulate from your mother, grandmother, or other influential women in your life. In order to prevent bitterness, see if you can come up with even one positive trait from within your immediate family. Using these characteristics as a framework, begin to form a plan, brainstorming with intention the type of mother you want to be. To this add characteristics and habits of other women you know. You can also seek out role models of mothers in books (biographies are good for this). Of course, if you can get to know some women who are further along the parenting journey than you are, even better. Everyone needs someone to consult for inspiration and advice at times. Remember that motherhood is a journey, and we all have issues to overcome. We don't have to be perfect, just willing to keep learning and growing.

2. I am divorced, working overtime, or in other difficult circumstances. How can I possibly have enthusiasm?

There are seasons in our lives when things don't seem steady and we are really struggling. It seems very blasé to say we should just "be happy" at these times. Sometimes post-partum or circumstantial depression creeps into our lives. We know these difficulties affect our children. Add in situations like a cross-country move, the loss of a job, a miscarriage, or a divorce, and you may have a lot of pain to deal with. There are no easy answers to such questions.

At such times it helps me to focus on just getting through each day, seeking to be as much of a stable force as possible in the midst of the stress that my children are also feeling. I find that functioning on a framework of a *Steady Routine* helps me when these types of serious difficulties arise. The loose structure enables me stay on emotional autopilot, maintaining a level of stability for the children even when challenging circumstances abound.

Also, I try not to beat myself up for having a difficult day. The snapshot of a single day, good or bad, does not define my life or my influence on my children—so let go of all that Mommy guilt! Rather, each day represents a small piece of a much larger and complex collage, with love as the unifying theme. I also think it's good for my children to see that we can support each other in the midst of life's ups and downs. Some days are difficult in their lives, too, and creating empathy in the home environment is a powerful message you send to them.

3. Help! I find myself juggling so many different roles and responsibilities that I lose my enthusiasm.

The pace of our Western lives these days can lead many parents to feel frazzled and forget any sense of rhythm. It is easy to over-commit, as there are so many wonderful opportunities out there for ourselves and our children. Sometimes, though, we miss out on the "best" if we can't say no to the "really good." When there are no quiet moments, no time to reflect, everyone in the family loses out on the special bonds created by peace and stability.

I find that often I begin emotionally running too fast without realizing it. The best way I have found to deal with this problem is to read the physical and emotional cues my body sends me when I'm beginning to run out of steam. Then the key is to respond. This could mean sleeping instead of working on that important project, making sure I'm eating enough of the right foods, or leaving the room for a few minutes before

I say something I might regret. If I'm careful to listen to these cues, I find I am able to maintain my sense of rhythm. Likewise, when I ignore the cues, my family and I pay the price for it.

This is a gradual process, and I am still on the journey. Mistakes are okay. They allow us to be vulnerable with our imperfections in front of our children. Apologies open the door to deepening relationships.

Part Three: Learning Together

*Education is not the filling of a
bucket, but the lighting of a fire.*

—William Butler Yeats

26. | Children Are Made to Learn

In the beginning of our children's lives, our focus as mothers is not typically on learning together, in the academic sense of the word. In reality, however, this is exactly what we are doing. From the first moment we set eyes on our child, the learning adventure begins.

In the first days and months after Jonathan came into our lives, I was consumed with learning what it meant to be a mom. Jonathan, of course, was learning about the new world he had entered. This was more than enough at the time. So I felt a little overwhelmed when I heard parents of older children discussing school choices or the best toys and television shows. I had no clue about any of that! There was an entire world that I had not yet explored, full of philosophies, advice, and information.

So I gleaned what I liked and didn't like from my friends and filed it away for a later day. I believe this is the best way to create our personal and professional mothering philosophy. We piece it together bit by bit, combining the information we learn with our own intuition and opinions. Don't be intimidated. Remember that no one knows your children better than you do.

A couple of years after Jonathan's birth, I heard about Charlotte Mason, a British educator in the late 1800s who revolutionized many of the educational practices in England at that time. She challenged the typical worldview of the value of children, how they learn, and their capabilities. At the same time that Charles Dickens was highlighting the exploitation of children through his novels, Mason brought to light similar issues in the educational realm.

Charlotte Mason believed that children are valid individuals who are created to learn and are gifted with a natural curiosity, no matter what their background or upbringing. She believed they are capable, whether poor or rich. She thought that they deserve to be treated with respect both by parents and by teachers. She spent four decades developing and putting her profound educational principles into practice in her schools.

While reading about her methods and thoughts regarding children, I experienced an inner "a-ha" moment. I had discovered a powerful method for relating to, and respecting, my children. One of Mason's ideas that is most relevant for professional mothers today is that parents are ultimately responsible for their children's education. No matter where children are enrolled in school, Mason thought, the nurturing of a child who loves learning begins and ends with the atmosphere at home. At the time in which she lived, rich parents in England hired governesses or sent their children to boarding schools. Poor parents often sent their children to work, unable to access education. Charlotte Mason challenged *both* of these groups, saying that neither one of them fully grasped the responsibility they held for their children's educations.

Mason stated that academic achievement is only one small measure of learning potential. She suggested that it is possible to maintain a child's natural curiosity and creativity, and that retaining the desire to learn throughout life was a more accurate measure of success than being a "good" student who makes the grade simply because he or she has learned to memorize well and work the system. She wrote, "The question is not,— how much does the youth know? when he has finished his education—but how much does he care? and about how many orders of things does he care? In fact, how large is the room in which he finds his feet set? and, therefore, how full is the life he has before him?"[6]

A number of more recent studies have confirmed Charlotte Mason's thoughts. One of the most intriguing was conducted by the National Assessment of Educational Progress. It found that there is a direct correlation between the amount of printed material (books, magazines, newspapers, etc.) in a child's home and the child's scores in reading, writing, and math. No matter where our children attend school, as mothers our involvement is one of the greatest factors determining their success.[7]

Many parents spend hours researching, visiting, and selecting a school for their child. Then they congratulate themselves on a job well done and think they've done their part. But choosing a good school is only the beginning. It's an admirable beginning, but it's not an end in and of itself. Good teachers are invaluable, good resources vital, good facilities wonderful. But without a parent who cares about learning alongside his or her child, these advantages can take a child only so far.

Charlotte Mason also wrote a great deal regarding the formation of habits in children, particularly in the early years of their lives. She believed that habits built in the early years will influence children later in life more than almost any other factor, both in their learning patterns and in their behavior. When I read Mason's thoughts on habits, they made complete sense to me. I had often found it amazing that almost every day I had the opportunity to create a new habit, either positive or negative, in my young children.

For example, once my husband and I took our two-year-old sons to a new children's museum. It was an incredible, imaginative place—a children's paradise. We had a wonderful time, and after we left, we went to a nearby restaurant for lunch. It was a special day together.

A few months later, I took the boys back to the museum, this time with a friend. Again we had a blast. As we were leaving, my son turned to me and said, "Mommy, are we going to the restaurant today?" I was surprised that he remembered from so long before.

In that moment, I realized I had the opportunity to form a habit. If I said yes and we went to the restaurant, from then on the museum alone would never be enough. It would always have to be "museum plus restaurant" in order to have the same fun effect. I could envision potential tantrums if I decided not to go to the restaurant after forming such a habit.

Now, there isn't necessarily anything wrong with forming the habit of always going to a restaurant after the museum. It may not be a *bad* habit. But I needed to *think* about it. I needed to be intentional and take a moment to decide. This is one of the biggest mistakes I think we as mothers make. It's all too easy to do things because it's the way we were raised, or the way our friends are doing it, and suddenly we find ourselves stuck with unpleasant habits in our children's sleep patterns, eating patterns, or behavior. We are the ones teaching and training our children, so we owe it to them to be purposeful.

Successful professionals don't happen by accident; they intentionally pursue success without being afraid of failure. Even if I make a mistake,

I'd rather it be something I'd given serious thought to, instead of something that happened because I neglected to consider the options.

So I told Jonathan, "No, we're not going to a restaurant today." He was fine with that, because the habit had not yet been formed. Since that time we've been back to that museum multiple times, and no one has mentioned the restaurant again. They've just enjoyed playing. But if someday I want to do something extra special, I can take them to a restaurant afterwards. This would be a real treat, and they would love it. The difference is that it isn't a *requirement*.

28. | Habits or Phases

When I mention habits, don't confuse these with phases. I've found that the two can sometimes be difficult to distinguish. Earlier in my career as a mother I had the false impression (based on too many books I had read) that following certain parenting formulas would produce children who behaved well almost all of the time and brought joy to all who were privileged enough to see them. I shudder to think of how I judged other parents when I saw their child throwing a tantrum or engaging in some other negative behavior. *My* children would be different!

Now I'm a little older and hopefully a little wiser. I'm definitely a little more experienced, at least. I'm raising children born on three different continents, yet—surprise, surprise—they're going through the same phases! This has helped me understand that children progress through developmental stages, and even unpleasant behaviors sometimes fit into that category. I have, unfortunately, spent time worrying about a behavior that, three months later, my child has outgrown.

I remember the screams of my youngest, Elijah, when he ran out of food and wanted more. There's nothing unusual about this for a nonverbal two-year-old, but it was very annoying. I taught him the sign language for "more" and this helped a little, but he didn't remember to use the sign every time. The scream came so much more naturally! I was convinced at the time that he would still be doing this when he was in his twenties. But less than a year later, Elijah has learned to say please when he wants something. Now he cries only half the time; the rest of the time he'll remember to ask nicely. This is life with children: constant training and teaching without always seeing an immediate result.

It can be hard to remember, but consistent reminding, modeling by example, and positive discipline will result in growth and the right habits in the end. And consistency doesn't have to mean doing the same thing in the same way every time. I think consistency in parenting means consistently being around, trying to be fully present when we are with our children, being observant and aware, and being involved. This is what sets the foundation for the learning and behavior that we hope to see in our children one day.

So why does a professional mother value learning with her children? The answer lies in examining your goals for your children. In my case, I want my little ones to grow into free-thinking, confident, and articulate individuals. I believe education is the gateway to reaching these goals. If they love learning, if they believe education happens not just during the school year but all their lives, then they will have the tools to discover and achieve, the tools to be self-motivated professionals themselves.

29. How Can We Learn Together?

The next question to ask is "How do we learn with our children?" This depends on you and your children, and *you* are the best one to answer it. One idea is to model the example in our own lives, in our work, hobbies, and interests. If we hope to create a learning lifestyle in our little ones, we have to display the continuing-education mindset ourselves.

Opportunities to do this often arise naturally. I like to leave the books I'm reading out where my children will see them. Books for both big and little people should have an important place in every learning home. We have books in our living room, dining room, and bedrooms, and often in the kitchen and bathrooms as well. My children think books are a natural, wonderful part of life, exactly the attitude I hope to cultivate. Often they will ask, "Mommy, what's this book about?" Sometimes they even add, "I want to read this one when I get bigger."

Our family subscribes to a mail-order DVD rental service. The children like to help me put the outgoing DVD in the mail slot of our front door. Sometimes they will ask which one I am returning. My husband and I enjoy documentaries, so this gives me an opportunity to explain a bit about what we learned the night before.

I hope to blur the line of *where* learning takes place. I grew up thinking that my education happened from September through May, seven hours a day. Outside of that time I could do what I *really* wanted. I was a good student, I learned to work the system, and I enjoyed some of my studies, but I didn't have an inner passion for learning. It didn't carry over into my personal life and interests. That's why my goal is to make learning together a family philosophy to pass on to my children, a continuous lifestyle that looks different depending on where we go, but always has the same goal in mind.

I also want to emphasize to my children that we are learning *together*. It's not just about me teaching them; we are joint companions on this learning adventure. If I can impart anything to them, it's as a guide and a facilitator, not as the one who knows it all.

I had a treat tonight as I was putting pajamas on my three-year-old. He told me he is glad that I am his mommy. Then he added, "You taught me everything I know!" This comment brought joy to this mother's heart. I was quick to remind him, though, that he has also taught me many things, and what is special about being in a family is that we get to learn together.

What should you learn with your children? There are so many options to consider. What material is your child studying in school that you can reinforce? This doesn't have to mean drilling the same information that your child is learning in class. It doesn't have to mean working on your child's "weak" area. Learning together requires creativity, curiosity, and effort.

Maybe your child is learning about the rainforest in science class. How can you help that come alive for your child? Try to show how subjects like science matter in real life. A textbook can take a child only so far, and often it isn't very far. But the resources and motivation of a caring parent can raise school concepts to the next level.

Travel is a wonderful way to make this happen. You don't have to fly to South America to see the rainforest firsthand (although can you imagine the lifelong impact a trip like that could have?). There are many state parks, wetlands, forests, and other locations nearby where nature can come alive for children. This, in essence, is the best type of field trip. So often we hear secondhand about our children's field trips, but how wonderful it is to be there with them. Finding avenues through which we can participate is a concrete way to show that we value who they are and what they are learning and that we want to be a part of it with them.

Children are fascinated by the world outside their immediate culture, if it is presented to them. Because of the diverse, international nature of our family, we are constantly discussing and bringing aspects of other countries into our lifestyle. As a result, it's not unusual to hear our children talking about Africa, the Philippines, or China. Even preschoolers can recognize and understand that they are part of a bigger world.

Any family can bring this global-mindedness to their home and can have endless opportunities for learning together. We keep a small map handy and locate any country we hear about or any place that is mentioned in a story we read. As the children get older, we place a high priority on traveling as a family, so the world can become real to them. It's more important to spend our money on this type of trip than any other vacation we could take, because it fits with our philosophy of learning together.

The most valuable opportunity to learn with our children is to follow their interests. Maybe there is something your child is fascinated by, but school hours aren't enough to cover what he or she wants to know. This is the open door to learning together, especially if you don't know the answers either. Suddenly you are not the expert, but a fellow participant in the process.

As children get older, they may want to learn practical skills like cooking, mechanics, or computer programming. After they learn, they can teach us. This gives us an opportunity to show respect for our children, builds confidence in them, and continues the learning adventure.

Don't be afraid to bring up something you're interested in learning. I've always wanted to know more about nature and have felt a little embarrassed that I didn't know the names of our local trees, flowers, and birds. I also hope that my children will learn to appreciate and be curious about nature at a young age. So I bought some nature guides, and we casually flip through them together. Now, when we see a new bird, one of the children will say, "What's the name of that bird, Mommy? Let's look it up in our book." Even more exciting is when we glimpse a new creature that we are able to identify *without* looking it up. In such moments, I feel a little surge of the joy that comes from learning something new.

Our children have so much to teach us. We have so much to teach them. Learning together truly is a *mutual* process that all members of the family get to be a part of. The effort required will yield so many dividends in our knowledge, our confidence, and our relationships with our children. I hope that the learning adventure never ends in our home, or in yours.

30. Steady Learning Board
(A Tool for Learning Together)

Remember bulletin boards in elementary school? Vivid colors and pictures conveying concepts to the children and brightening up the classroom. I remember both looking at them as a student and putting them together later in life. The *Steady Learning Board* is a bulletin board made the best way, by you and your children. It is specific to your needs and learning goals.

Sometimes mothers who work outside of the home aren't able to see firsthand what their children learn each day in childcare, preschool, or elementary school. Often, though, daycares or schools send out newsletters to communicate the concepts children will learn in the coming week or month. These concepts, or any of your own initiative, are the impetus behind the *Steady Learning Board*. Use it to highlight and remind your children about what they are learning throughout the day. Print, draw, and color pictures and stick them on. Make it a family activity.

We also use our Learning Board to hang items that inspire us—photos, magazine clippings, treasures the children find outside. It's easy to learn from the things we find beautiful.

You can make your *Steady Learning Board* from simple posterboard or from a sturdier, nicely framed board. Hang it anywhere your child will regularly see it. We keep ours in the dining room, and at every meal, at least one of our children will mention the letter, number, or poem they've been learning—it's a gentle way to emphasize whatever our children are studying during the day.

Clearly this isn't a new concept, but it's an effective one. That's why the bulletin board has been around for so long. Why make one? To watch your child learn, to see a spark excite them as they catch a new concept and share it with you. It blurs the line between school and home. And don't we hope our children will discover that true learning happens anytime, anywhere? This is one simple way to step toward that goal.

Want to make your own *Steady Learning Board?* These items might help:

Bulletin Board or Poster Board

Suggested topics and items:

* Numbers
* Letters
* Poetry
* Scripture verses
* Holidays
* Seasons
* Colors
* Shapes
* Countries
* Authors
* Maps
* Math formulas
* Parts of speech
* Vocabulary words
* Items that inspire you

Our Learning Board brings a gentle learning atmosphere to our home.

31. *Steady Learning Scrapbook*
(A Tool for Learning Together)

The *Steady Learning Scrapbook* can be used in conjunction with your Learning Board. As you remove items from your board to add new ones, your children can select their favorites, glue them onto a sheet of cardstock, and insert them into their Learning Scrapbook. The Scrapbook will grow over time and become a picture book that your children can flip through when they like—a natural, unforced way to review material.

After doing this with our children, my husband and I realized we wanted to have our own Learning Scrapbooks. In my book I keep photocopies and notes from the books I've been reading, my goals for the year, thoughts from lectures and conferences I've attended, and ideas for new topics I want to study in the future. This allows for brainstorming and intentional direction in my learning, keeps inspiration flowing, and serves as a reminder of subjects I'm curious about. The children also like to include souvenirs from educational trips we've taken in their Scrapbooks.

Your kids can also have Learning Scrapbook sections called "Things I Want to Know" and "Things I'm Learning Now." As a mother, this gives insight into what your children are interested, providing guidance as you gather ideas to delve into with them. When your kids begin exploring a topic from the first section, they then transfer the materials they produce to the second section. As children get older, the Scrapbook is also an excellent place to keep study guides, test schedules, and other school papers.

We keep our Learning Scrapbooks on an easily accessible shelf where any family member can take a look. They represent part of the family culture we're trying to create, where learning is a natural part of living.

Having a *Steady Learning Scrapbook* in your home is a visual demonstration to children that education occurs throughout all of life and that it's an exciting privilege to continue growing in knowledge no matter how old you are.

Want to make *Learning Scrapbooks* for your family? These items might help:

3-ring Binder(s)   Plastic Page Protectors

You can find a blank sample of this resource in Appendix A and at www.steadydays.com.

A sample page from Trishna's Learning Scrapbook.

32. Questions & Answers—Learning Together

1. What if I don't enjoy reading with my children?

Reading is one of my passions, so it has naturally evolved to be an important part of my family's life. But this is not the case for everyone. Recently my friend Angie mentioned that it has been challenging for her to get into a rhythm of regular story time with her children. Yet she feels it's important. She believes it will help develop their creativity, imagination, and love of learning. Angie also feels reading and listening together provide a natural opportunity to bond. She said that setting aside a specific time of day has helped her develop the reading habit.

Some mothers feel uncomfortable reading aloud, and therefore are reluctant to do so. For these individuals, I suggest practicing with short intervals and books to get started. Also, you can find children's audio books that you can enjoy together without having to read yourself.

Not all books are created equal, and not all children's books stimulate creativity and imagination. Look for quality, not necessarily what is currently on the bestseller list. Consult Appendix B for recommended resources to help you choose excellent reading material.

2. What if my child's school does not seem to be fulfilling his or her learning needs?

It's easy to feel helpless and out of options if the local school system isn't meeting your family's needs. But as Charlotte Mason said, no matter where children go to school, it's ultimately we as parents who are responsible for their education. So we have to be involved and be intentional.

One option is to supplement your child's education at home. This is becoming popular enough to have its own term: afterschooling. This doesn't mean that your child arrives home after a full day and has more structured lessons. A child who has been at school all day needs decompression time upon arriving home. But you can create a natural learning environment by having interesting materials easily accessible. It can be as simple as reading a gripping novel together while eating a snack.

Open the doors for learning and curiosity to develop at home even if they're being stifled at school.

It's also important to realize that we always have choices. Changing nothing is still making a choice. This realization helps us avoid feeling helpless in the face of challenges. In my case, I researched all of the options available to decide what was best for my children's education. This wasn't a one-time decision, but will be ongoing as the children grow. These days we are privileged to have many educational options: public schools, private schools, homeschools, magnet schools, co-op schools, and more. If your child isn't thriving where he or she is, don't be afraid to investigate other ideas.

3. I don't have a college degree. Does this mean I can't be a professional mother or learn with my children?

Being a professional mother has everything to do with the right mindset and philosophy and little to do with degrees or qualifications. If your goal is to purposefully give your children the best start and if you're willing to consider and try different approaches, then you are a professional mother.

Each professional mother has unique talents to pass on to her children. We begin the learning adventure the minute they enter our lives. Even though we make mistakes, we can always start again with renewed enthusiasm and intention. Even the most qualified, experienced teacher is not as committed to our children's success as we are. Therefore, we are their best teachers. So let's be confident.

Part Four: Making Memories

God gave us memory so that we might have roses in December.

—J. M. Barrie

33. | Meeting Our Children

Who could ever forget the first time they saw their child? I became a mother in a Texan hospital after a full day of labor. When the doctor placed the grayish blob that was Jonathan on my chest, I was in awed shock. Even though I was exhausted, I couldn't sleep that night. Adrenaline pumped through me as I stared at my baby. I remember thinking, "This is forever, and I don't have a clue what I'm doing."

My husband and I were soon struck by how much our little newborn required of us, and this realization led us to consider the many children around the world who don't have parents. We never expected it to happen as quickly as it did, but just over a year after Jonathan was born, I became a mother again. This time it was an entirely different experience.

My husband, Steve, stayed with Jonathan at our home in Texas as I embarked on two days of travel alone. Finally I arrived in Liberia, West Africa, late at night and collapsed into bed at the hotel. The next morning I stood, bewildered by jet lag, in the damp heat of a crowded orphanage. Children, ranging from infants to school age, danced and sang as they welcomed our group. As the music played, the orphanage director danced toward me and placed in my arms my six-month-old son, Elijah.

It wasn't clear if our new little one, sick with malaria and parasites, would make it. I was alone in a poverty-stricken country, separated from my husband and my thirteen-month-old. After our two-day journey to return to the United States, Elijah was admitted to a children's hospital where the treatment saved his life. Today he is an incredibly healthy and active boy, with a dimpled smile that melts hearts.

Our third child joined the family in mid-2007. My husband and I nervously paced the floor in our hotel room before being taken to meet our daughter in Pune, India. I had been sick all night from food poisoning and desperately wanted to crawl back into bed for the day. It was far from the ideal memory I had hoped to make. Exhausted and still very ill, I wondered if I could handle the challenge ahead. Questions ran through my mind, including "What do you do when you meet your four-year-old for the first time, particularly when she speaks another language?"

The children at the orphanage ran around calling, "Trishna's mommy and daddy are here!" Trishna, of course, was a bit more hesitant to jump into the arms of strangers. We spent the day soaking up every detail of the place our daughter had called home for many years, forming images in our minds to pass on later. Looking back, I can see that the many fragments of our trip, including my sickness, have become embedded in our family's story. All the details combine to create a memorable tapestry, one that will remain with us forever.

No matter where we meet our little ones for the first time, the experience becomes etched in our minds. It changes us, and the memories are ones we treasure. How blessed mothers are that this profound start is only the *beginning* of a lifetime of memory-making with our children.

34. Follow the Spark

Recently we went through several weeks that were far from memorable. There was a general blahness to our days. An undercurrent of boredom among the children led to more disciplinary situations than usual. We were following our *Steady Routine*, but the passion was missing. I felt I was dragging myself through much of it; it wasn't flowing or coming naturally. So I took some time to consider both the problem and a potential solution. Suddenly a phrase came to mind, reminding me to "follow the spark."

Just as there are times for creating and implementing routines, there are also times to inject flexibility and spontaneity into our lives. The spark is what had been missing from our routine. A professional mother recognizes when she needs a change and isn't afraid to experiment with new ideas.

Some mornings, we wake up and immediately consider all we need to accomplish. Then we glance out the window and see a glorious day unfolding. That's the perfect time to forget what needs to be done, when we can, and follow the spark. Build a castle, gather flowers, have a picnic, go to an amusement park—whatever strikes our fancy. Often it's the unexpected that creates memories.

Because my children are close in age, when they were younger I was hesitant to take them to certain places alone. I worried that maybe I wouldn't be able to handle it. This concern, while legitimate, had begun to dampen the spark in all of us. I realized that even if we stayed for only a few minutes, we had still followed the spark, and the effort would rejuvenate all of us.

So for a couple of weeks we followed the essential segments of our *Steady Routine*, but then we piled in the van and set out for adventure. We headed to new museums, ate ice cream, explored new parks, and had a blast. It warmed my heart to watch my children playing for hours in the waves and sand of a local beach, where previously I would have gone only if I had help. Their faces shone with contagious wonder as they brought me shells, seaweed, and other treasures to examine. Having a new experience helped them listen and respond better, and we all felt refreshed afterwards. I also gained confidence by seeing that, in the right situations, I could take all three children to places that I had previously thought too challenging.

After those two weeks, we returned to our *Steady Routine* with joy because we had followed the spark. But now I've added one week each month to our flexible routine to gain new inspiration. My goal is to include more of the unexpected and hopefully avoid getting into another rut later. I want to retain an atmosphere in my home that is conducive to making memories, while still accomplishing the necessary tasks that make daily life flow smoothly.

35. Family Traditions and the Long-Term Goal

Traditions form the cornerstone of memories. My mom and I still sometimes say, "Do you want to share an orange?" This refers back to a tradition we had of eating oranges and watching *Sesame Street* together, one of my earliest and most vivid memories. Traditions don't have to be unusual or expensive, as this example illustrates. They just have to be intentional, which is the most important quality of a professional mother.

As well as the simple daily traditions, special yearly traditions stay with us. When I was growing up, my dad took me out every year on the Saturday before my birthday. I have no idea how this tradition began, but I will never forget the adventures we had together. I got to plan the itinerary for my day (within reason). We usually bought a birthday present and had lunch together. My dad passed away several years ago, so I cherish these memories even more now.

All of us have holiday traditions we remember from our early years. How exciting to be in the position to thoughtfully create traditions for our own families.

Traditions and rituals can vary from child to child, so tailor them to your child's personality and interests. My husband recently began a Friday ritual of bringing Jonathan a picture of a garbage truck he had printed out during his workday. Garbage trucks are my son's current passion, and as soon as Steve walks in the door on Fridays, the first words out of Jonathan's mouth are "Did you bring me a garbage truck picture?" After dinner when my husband gives it to him, Jonathan practically shakes with excitement. Then they go upstairs to take down the previous week's picture and tape up the new one. This is the highlight of Jonathan's week.

You don't need a list of suggested traditions to implement. There are no right or wrong answers for creating your family's memories. If you follow your spark and your child's spark, many opportunities will present themselves.

The Long-Term Goal

Several years ago when I was pregnant with Jonathan, I was taking a walk around the block where we lived. It was a quiet afternoon, and I passed by the house where our friends Wade and Sharon lived with their three young children. Suddenly Wade dashed out from behind a parked car, running and shouting like a madman. Then his young daughter appeared, screaming with delight and surprise as she tried to run away. It was impossible to watch the scene without smiling and laughing.

Later I mentioned to Wade what I had seen and the fun of being an unnoticed observer. He replied, "I try to keep in mind that at every moment with my children I have the power to make a memory." Even though I didn't have any kids, his comment stayed with me.

A lifetime of memories helps our little ones feel grounded and gives them a foundation from which to become independent. As a professional mother, I believe I am raising a future friend. I look forward to a deepening relationship with my children as adults, still continuing to make memories together.

36. Look at Me Binder
(A Tool for Making Memories)

The early childhood years pass all too quickly. It's hard to imagine, but soon our little ones won't be so little anymore. Some mothers love scrapbooking, spending hours arranging their children's photos and special papers in elaborately decorated albums. That has never been my talent or passion.

But it wasn't long after my children came along that I realized paper clutter had taken on a whole new meaning. Particularly after children reach toddlerhood, their homes begin to overflow with artwork, school papers to sign, and tests being returned. Items our children spent hours preparing may end up tossed in a box or the trash, unless we come up with a system to keep track of it all. We need an easy, practical, and professional way to keep up with our children's materials.

In the end I decided that I don't have to save it all, but what I do keep should be kept well. So I started a *Look at Me Binder* for each of our children. Our three kids produce piles of paintings and drawings every week. And they are preschoolers—I can only imagine what is to come. I keep an eye out for the masterpieces that really convey their personalities at the time. This way their memory book becomes a true snapshot of who they are becoming.

My youngest, Elijah, loves painting, spreading colors with his fingers over the entire page. He's also developed a drumming technique with his paintbrushes that would rival that of the Blue Man Group. Usually when I ask Elijah what he's painted, he says, "A picture." But one day, he went to great lengths with both his limited vocabulary and his hands to communicate that it was a fish. And he didn't stop there. He continued gesturing with his arms, flapping, until I caught on that it was a flying fish. When I finally got it, he said, "Yep," his face glowing with an artist's satisfaction. His certainty, imagination, and perseverance made it a definite entry for his *Look at Me Binder*.

I've also included handprints of my children at certain ages, and a painting to represent the day my daughter, Trishna, finally started making rainbows instead of mixing all the colors to make brown.

The *Look at Me Binder* is simple. You insert items when you first have your hands on them. There is no preparation required and no extra creativity necessary. When you have a photo or piece of schoolwork you want to keep for your child, quickly jot down any memorable information (date, child's age, occasion) on the back, slide it into a page protector or photo holder, and insert it into the binder. You can also have your children do their project directly on the Sample Look at Me Page* if you know in advance that it will be an item you want to keep.

The binder will grow along with your children, and you can present it to them on the day they graduate, move out, get married, or at another special event. My personal goal is to be able to give each of my children a book of memories without having to spend any sleepless nights getting it ready. I value this tool because when it's completed, many years from now, it will be a tangible representation of my love for them and of their amazing and unique giftedness. It will contain a lifetime of memories in one book—a beautiful treasure to pass on.

Want to make a *Look at Me Binder?* These items might help:

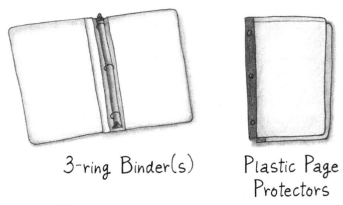

3-ring Binder(s)   Plastic Page Protectors

*You can find the Sample Look at Me Page in Appendix A and at www.steadydays.com.

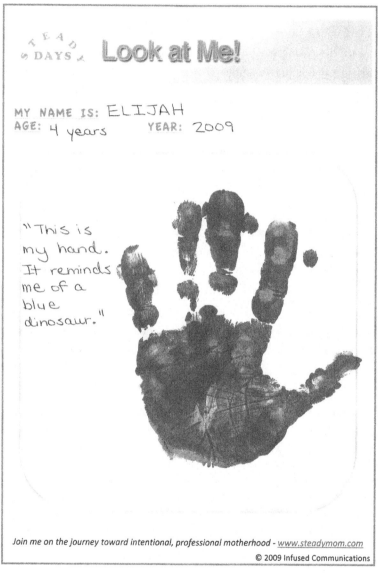

Handprints at various ages are perfect additions to a Look at Me Binder.

37. Mom's Favorite Moments
(A Tool for Making Memories)

It started with a phone call to my mother. I was explaining that Jonathan and I were discussing what he wants to be when he grows up. His response? "A garbage truck driver and a kazoo player!" Laughing, my mom said, "I hope you're writing all of these comments down somewhere." After I got off the phone, I started thinking. I should be writing these memories down. But what method should I use? The subsequent brainstorming led to the creation of my *Mom's Favorite Moments* book.

Here's my system: Each child has one to two pages per year in a binder. On the front of each page I place one or more of my favorite photos of the child from that year. I often pick photos taken on the child's birthday. On the back of the page, I write down memorable comments the child said, as well as any special activities and events I want to remember from that year. I keep the current year's page for each child in my *Steady Home Planner* so I can add comments easily. At the end of the year I transfer this to my *Mom's Favorite Moments* book. You can either use one large binder with dividers for all your children or purchase one small binder for each child.

The *Look at Me Binder* will one day belong to my child, but the *Mom's Favorite Moments* book is a keepsake for me. Memories contain both power and beauty. I love to imagine the day when these binders are full of the rich, unique, and valuable life we have shared together. To remember is to see how far we've come and the challenges we've made it through, and to savor the love we've been privileged to share.

Want to make a *Mom's Favorite Moments Book*? These items might help:

Plastic Page Protectors

3-ring Binder(s)

You can find a blank Sample Mom's Favorite Moments Page in Appendix A and at www.steadydays.com.

Mom's Favorite Moments

NAME: Jonathan
AGE: 3 years   YEAR: 2007 - 2008

My Jonathan —
A sweet, sensitive
Boy

professional motherhood - www.steadymom.com

© 2009 Infused Communications

This sample shows my favorite memories of Jonathan at three-years-old.

THINGS YOU SAID:

* Referred to Trishna as "Jonathan's Favorite Sister"
* "I really like Mommy."
* "I see USA flag - Daddy's favorite flag!"
* "Mommy, we have a nice family, don't we."
* As an order: "Mommy - come dance with me!"
* Told me you loved me for the very first time (after a stressful day of potty training)

THINGS YOU DID:

* You + I went for a special solo date before your birthday - to the animal park + ice cream
* Celebrated Autumn at the Pumpkin Farm - you had your first pony ride and loved it!
* Moved into a big-kid bed

THINGS YOU LIKE:

* Learning about nature - Venus Flytrap is your favorite plant.
* GARBAGE TRUCKS - your passion!
* You love broccoli, + always eat it first.
* You love to read Bible stories.

Join me on the journey toward intentional, professional motherhood - www.steadymom.com

© 2009 Infused Communications

38. | Questions & Answers—Making Memories

1. I'm not sentimental and I've always thought that if I didn't keep pictures and memories in my mind, they weren't worth saving. What do you think?

I can relate. I don't particularly enjoy taking a camera everywhere and prefer to focus on being present in the moment instead of trying to photographically document every event. There's a balance to strike in this regard. Even though I feel that way about *taking* pictures, I really love *looking* at pictures of myself when I was a child.

I try to remind myself that my children may feel this way one day as well. I want to ensure they will be able to see our lives during this time. It's a special gift I can give to them.

2. Life is very difficult right now in our family. I find I'm apathetic toward remembering this time; I am just trying to survive it.

This is a legitimate and common way to feel. Stressful circumstances in our lives can make us wish the time would pass quickly so we can enter an easier season. For my children's sake, though, I feel it's best if I live in the moment, even in painful times. I don't believe we have to pretend it isn't painful; we don't have to fake it. At the same time we can also make an effort to focus on the positive and be thankful where we can. These are character traits we hope to pass on to our children, and what better way and place to model them than in the face of adversity?

It is easy, especially in the labor-intensive early years with children, to look forward to when they will be more independent. But with that independence comes new challenges. My friends with older children often comment that as their children grow older the issues don't necessarily become easier; they are just different. We can end up constantly daydreaming about greener grass that doesn't really exist. My husband and I remind ourselves of this during difficult times by saying that no matter what is going on, "It doesn't get any better than this." This is a reminder for us to focus on the now and revel in the present. We owe it to our children to keep trying. Even in difficult circumstances, we can survive and continue hoping for the future.

3. Do I need to make new traditions with my children, or should I just pass down those from my younger years?

It's a beautiful thing to see traditions handed down through generations. One of my favorite memories while growing up was having cinnamon rolls for breakfast each Christmas morning—I've adapted this ritual for our family and the children love it.

Don't feel pressured to keep *all* the traditions you had as a child. Between you and your spouse you probably have many to choose from. Pick your favorites and experiment with them inside your home.

Blending old and new traditions is an exciting part of building your family. New traditions will probably present themselves without much planning. If you could use a few ideas and inspiration, consult Appendix B for suggested resources.

39. | A Mother with a Mission

About a year ago, my husband came home from work and told me about a new process he was following in order to develop a personal and professional vision statement. I listened, skeptical. "Can't we just live in the moment?" I thought. We don't need to box ourselves into something that may or may not happen.

Not wanting to sound discouraging, I kept these words to myself. But over time, as Steve worked through the process, I found myself becoming thoughtful about my own vision and interested in putting some of my ideas down in writing.

Here's an overview of the steps I followed to create a mission and vision statement. Use them in whatever order appeals as you consider one of your own.

1. Make a list of your current priorities: children, husband, outside jobs, values, passions, faith, etc. What are the things closest to your heart at this time?

2. List your talents, skills, education, and life experiences.

3. Brainstorm a few current and future goals. Think about what excites you and get it down on paper. Writing them down doesn't mean you *will* do all of these things, but it will get you thinking about what is possible.

   Group your goals into various time segments: one to three years, three to five years, five to ten years, and ten to fifteen years from now. Dividing my future goals into these categories has helped to compartmentalize my thinking. Recently, for example, I found an incredible master's degree program that I would love to enroll in. It connects with my vision, mission, and priorities. Yet I know that it isn't the right season in my life to start a master's degree. So instead I entered it into my list of three- to five-year goals.

   There was a time when I might have felt resentful that I couldn't begin a project like that now. But since I began keeping my vision and goals list, my perspective of time is more balanced. I can visualize what is important right now and what can wait. Time doesn't

Part Four: Making Memories   111

seem so long anymore. This helps me feel empowered by what I am doing and not frustrated by what I can't do. Instead I can imagine the time when my goals will fit and work for the family.

4. Examine your lists for similar themes or threads. There may be one, two, or many. I was surprised to see that in many different ways and avenues in life, I am motivated by the desire to help children. Although this thread has been present for my entire life, I had never made the connection. Now, for the first time, I have discovered my life's mission. It's part of what I've done in the past, part of what I'm currently doing in my home with my children, and part of my goals for the future. This led to the crafting of my mission statement, "To empower, educate, and seek justice for children."

5. Using your mission statement as inspiration, write a longer vision statement. It should be a few paragraphs that incorporate where you are and where you hope to go in the future. These words should inspire you, challenge you, and keep you energized.

I finished my first mission and vision statements over a year ago, and they continue to undergo slight revisions. Every time I read them, I get excited! I love what I'm doing right now, and I love imagining what is to come.

Having defined and refined my vision and mission means I have a real sense of purpose behind what I do. Even small things, like changing a diaper, fit into the big perspective when viewed this way. Therefore it's easier to accept them without frustration. Every task is valid because everything is part of the big picture.

Companies and organizations spend significant time and money developing their own extensive vision statements. Let's use the same model of efficiency and mindfulness in our careers as mothers.

There are many resources to help you draft and process your own mission and vision statements. Consult Appendix B for further recommendations.

40. Principles, Not Tools

A professional mother isn't perfect and can admit to herself and others when she's made a mistake. Professionalism is not about achieving a desired result but is about living with purpose and focus. When we live with intention, we invest in our future and the future of our children.

The professional mother holds the underlying knowledge that when it comes to her children, *she* is the only expert. How many of us have spent too much time poring over parenting books, turning the last page only to feel inadequate to do all the author requires? Often we read conflicting opinions and do not know which one to believe. I've found myself in this situation before and have finally realized that no matter how popular a book or author may be, the techniques just may not be right for my family and my children.

Children are unique individuals and will not necessarily conform to what a certain bestseller says. As mothers, we are the ones with the intuition and wisdom about what will work for our little ones. A professional mother can go with her gut, even if it's unpopular and even if she's a little unsure. What works for one family will be quite different than what works for another. That is the beauty of variety, the beauty of owning our personal path, the beauty of caring for our children. In times of inner conflict or indecision, just remember—you are the expert!

So what happens when the expert makes a mistake? As previously mentioned, expertise is not the same as perfection. This is why an atmosphere of grace can transform our homes and our lives. Just as we aim to be patient with our children, we must choose patience with ourselves. My children have helped me learn this lesson many times. There have been many times when I've needed to apologize for getting angry or making a mistake. Their eagerness to show grace often surprises me, as they wrap little arms around me and say, "That's okay, Mommy." Always present in the moment, they never hold a grudge. I want to live the same way, showing grace toward others and myself.

I will always have personality weaknesses and other flaws to work on as a professional mother. I will never "arrive." Motherhood is a journey and I'm on the path, with the freedom to keep growing and changing. With grace in my life, I am able to leave the past behind me and move with expectancy into the future. This is an important lesson I want to model for my children.

I hope the tools and thoughts in *Steady Days* have been of use to you. But keep in mind that *Steady Days* is really about principles, not tools. The relevance of the specific tools and ideas in this manual to your current phase of life will come and go. These suggested tools are not the keys to Steady Days; there is nothing magical about them by themselves. Instead it's the *principles* of getting organized, retaining enthusiasm, learning together, and making memories that will lead to Steady Days with your children. These principles empower you to do your job efficiently, effectively, and joyously. But the *application* of the principles will change as you journey forward with your children.

So use *Steady Days* to your advantage. Modify the techniques to suit your family's lifestyle, your career, and your children. And if one of the tools ceases to be of use, put it aside and create a new one. Seek out something fresh when it's needed, while still maintaining the same principles. I am not the expert; you are. Be confident in your chosen profession as a mother, and enjoy the adventure.

Appendix A
Steady Days Documents

This appendix includes blank copies of the specific documents I refer to throughout the book. You are welcome to copy and enlarge them or use them for ideas to create your own resources.

You can also affordably purchase and download print-ready, editable copies of these ten forms at www.steadydays.com.

* *Steady Routine* Draft Worksheet
* Dates to Remember Organizer
* *Steady Blessings*—For Moms
* *Steady Blessings*—For Kids
* *Steady Blessings*—For Moms & Kids
* Sample *Steady Thoughts*
* My *Learning Scrapbook* Page
* *Look at Me Binder* Page
* *Mom's Favorite Moments* Page
* Mission/Vision Statement Worksheet

Steady Routine
Draft Worksheet

STEADY DAYS A Steady Routine

TIME/ DURATION	MOM			
Morning				
Afternoon				

Join me on the journey toward intentional, professional motherhood - www.steadymom.com

Evening				

Join me on the journey toward intentional, professional motherhood - www.steadymom.com

© 2009 Infused Communications

Appendix A: *Steady Days* Documents **117**

Dates to
Remember Organizer

STEADY DAYS Dates to Remember

January

February

March

April

May

June

July

August

September

October

November

December

Join me on the journey toward intentional, professional motherhood - www.steadymom.com

Steady Blessings—
For Moms

Mom's Steady Blessings

S·T·E·A·D·Y DAYS

DATE:

DATE:

DATE:

Join me on the journey toward intentional, professional motherhood - www.steadymom.com

© 2009 Infused Communications

Steady Blessings—
For Kids

My Steady Blessings

STEADY DAYS

DATE:

Today I'm thankful for...

Join me on the journey toward intentional, professional motherhood - www.steadymom.com

Steady Blessings—
For Moms & Kids

STEADY DAYS — **Our Steady Blessings**

DATE:

Today I'm thankful for...

_____

_____

_____

Today I'm thankful for...

Sample
Steady Thoughts

Inspiring Quotations

1. The world is a great book, of which they who never stir from home read only a page. *(Saint Augustine)*

2. Write down the thought of the moment. Those that come unsought for are commonly the most valuable. *(Francis Bacon)*

3. The secret of happiness is not in doing what one likes, but in liking what one has to do. *(J.M. Barrie)*

4. I love to think of nature as an unlimited broadcasting system, through which God speaks to us every hour, if we will only tune in. *(George Washington Carver)*

5. There are two ways to get enough. One is to continue to accumulate more and more. The other is to desire less and less. *(G.K. Chesterton)*

6. If you have a garden and a library, you have everything you need. *(Marcus Tullius Cicero)*

7. I love these little people, and it is not a slight thing when they who are fresh from God love us. *(Charles Dickens)*

8. If we did all the things we are capable of doing, we would literally astonish ourselves. *(Thomas Edison)*

9. Guard your spare moments. They are like uncut diamonds. Discard them and their value will never be known. Improve them and they will become the brightest gems in a useful life. *(Ralph Waldo Emerson)*

10. Though we travel the world over to find the beautiful, we must carry it with us, or we find it not. *(Ralph Waldo Emerson)*

11. The joy we seek is not a temporary emotional high but a habitual inner joy learned from long experience and trust in God. *(James Faust)*

12. Dost thou love life? Then do not squander time, for that is the stuff life is made of. *(Benjamin Franklin)*

13. If you would not be forgotten as soon as you are gone, either write things worth reading or do things worth writing. *(Benjamin Franklin)*

14. I will not let anyone walk through my mind with their dirty feet. *(Mahatma Gandhi)*

15. The man who is born with a talent which he is meant to use finds his greatest happiness in using it. *(Johann von Goethe)*

16. The more we do, the more we can do; the more busy we are, the more leisure we have. *(William Hazlitt)*

17. Adversity has the effect of eliciting talents which in prosperous circumstances would have lain dormant. *(Horace)*

18. There is nothing as powerful as an idea whose time has come. *(Victor Hugo)*

19. To be happy at home is the ultimate result of all ambition. *(Samuel Johnson)*

20. Great tranquility of heart is for he who cares for neither praise nor blame. *(Thomas a Kempis)*

21. If we could read the secret history of our enemies, we should find in each man's life, sorrow and suffering enough to disarm all hostility. *(Henry Wadsworth Longfellow)*

22. It is well we should recognize that the business of education is with us all our lives, that we must always go on increasing our knowledge. *(Charlotte Mason)*

23. Let us do each bit of work as perfectly as we know how, remembering that each thing we turn out is a bit of ourselves, and we must leave it whole and complete, for this is Integrity. *(Charlotte Mason)*

24. In the rush and noise of life, as you have intervals, be still. Wait upon God and feel His good presence; this will carry you evenly through your day's business. *(William Penn)*

25. The first and best victory is to conquer self. *(Plato)*

26. The haunts of happiness are varied, but I have more often found her among little children, home firesides, and country houses than anywhere else. *(Sydney Smith)*

27. May you live all the days of your life. *(Jonathan Swift)*

28. If one advances confidently in the direction of his dreams, and endeavors to live the life which he imagined, he will meet with a success unexpected in common hours. *(Henry David Thoreau)*

29. Twenty years from now you will be more disappointed by the things you didn't do than by the ones you did do. So throw off the bowlines. Sail away from the safe harbor. Catch the trade winds in your sails. Explore. Dream. Discover. *(Mark Twain)*

30. After you have sought over the wide world, you learn that happiness is to be found only in your own home. *(Voltaire)*

31. We are all in the gutter, but some of us are looking at the stars. *(Oscar Wilde)*

Scriptural Meditations

(all verses are from the New Living Translation of the Bible)

1. The Lord gives his people strength. The Lord blesses them with peace. (Psalm 29:11)

2. I prayed to the Lord, and he answered me, freeing me from all my fears. (Psalm 34:4)

3. Taste and see that the Lord is good. Oh, the joys of those who trust in Him! (Psalm 34:8)

4. God is our refuge and strength, always ready to help in times of trouble. (Psalm 46:1)

5. My health may fail, and my spirit may grow weak, but God remains the strength of my heart; He is mine forever. (Psalm 73:26)

6. This is the day the Lord has made. We will rejoice and be glad in it. (Psalm 118:24)

7. You chart the path ahead of me and tell me where to stop and rest. Every moment you know where I am. You both precede and follow me. You place your hand of blessing on my head. (Psalm 139:3,5)

8. A gentle answer turns away wrath, but harsh words stir up anger. (Proverbs 15:1)

9. For the happy heart, life is a continual feast. (Proverbs 15:15)

10. Kind words are like honey—sweet to the soul and healthy for the body. (Proverbs 16:24)

11. Disregarding another person's faults preserves love; telling about them separates close friends. (Proverbs 17:9)

12. A cheerful heart is good medicine, but a broken spirit saps a person's strength. (Proverbs 17:22)

13. You will keep in perfect peace all who trust in you, whose thoughts are fixed on you! (Isaiah 26:3)

14. Those who wait on the Lord will find new strength. They will fly high on wings like eagles. They will run and not grow weary. They will walk and not faint. (Isaiah 40:31)

15. Don't be afraid, for I am with you. Do not be dismayed, for I am your God. I will strengthen you. I will help you. (Isaiah 41:10)

16. God blesses those who work for peace, for they will be called the children of God. (Matthew 5:9)

17. So don't worry about tomorrow, for tomorrow will bring its own worries. Today's trouble is enough for today. (Matthew 6:34)

18. Come to me, all of you who are weary and carry heavy burdens, and I will give you rest. (Matthew 11:28)

19. With God everything is possible. (Matthew 19:26)

20. My purpose is to give life in all its fullness. (John 10:10)

21. I am leaving you with a gift—peace of mind and heart. And the peace I give isn't like the peace the world gives. So don't be troubled or afraid. (John 14:27)

22. If God is for us, who can ever be against us? (Romans 8:31)

23. My gracious favor is all you need. My power works best in your weakness. (2 Corinthians 12:9)

24. Be humble and gentle. Be patient with each other, making allowance for each other's faults because of your love. (Ephesians 4:2)

25. Work with enthusiasm, as though you were working for the Lord rather than for people. (Ephesians 6:7)

26. For I can do everything with the help of Christ who gives me the strength I need. (Philippians 4:13)

27. And this same God who takes care of me will supply all your needs from his glorious riches, which have been given to us in Christ Jesus. (Philippians 4:19)

28. Work hard and cheerfully at whatever you do, as though you were working for the Lord rather than for people. (Colossians 3:23)

29. No matter what happens, always be thankful. (1 Thessalonians 5:18)

30. For God has not given us a spirit of fear and timidity, but of power, love, and self-discipline. (2 Timothy 1:7)

31. Be quick to listen, slow to speak, and slow to get angry. Your anger can never make things right in God's sight. (James 1:19-20)

My *Learning Scrapbook* Page

STEADY DAYS

My Learning Scrapbook

I'VE LEARNED ABOUT...

MY NAME IS:

Join me on the journey toward intentional, professional motherhood - www.steadymom.com

© 2009 Infused Communications

Look at Me
Binder Page

Mom's Favorite Moments Page

STEADY DAYS — Mom's Favorite Moments

NAME:

AGE: YEAR:

Place Photo Here

_____

_____

_____

_____

Join me on the journey toward intentional, professional motherhood - www.steadymom.com

© 2009 Infused Communications

THINGS YOU SAID:

_____

_____

_____

_____

_____

_____

THINGS YOU DID:

_____

_____

_____

_____

_____

THINGS YOU LIKE:

_____

_____

_____

_____

_____

Join me on the journey toward intentional, professional motherhood - www.steadymom.com

Mission/Vision Statement Worksheet

 Mission & Vision Statements

CURRENT PRIORITIES

Make a list of your current priorities: children, husband, outside jobs, values, passions, faith, etc. What are the things closest to your heart at this time?

1. _____

2. _____

3. _____

4. _____

5. _____

6. _____

7. _____

8. _____

9. _____

10. _____

Join me on the journey toward intentional, professional motherhood - www.steadymom.com

SKILL SETS

List your talents, skills, education, and life experiences.

1.

2.

3.

4.

5.

6.

7.

8.

9.

10.

GOAL SETTING

Brainstorm a few current and future goals. Group your goals into various time segments: 1-3 years, 3-5 years, 5-10 years, and 10-15 years from now.

1-3 YEARS:

Join me on the journey toward intentional, professional motherhood - www.steadymom.com

3-5 YEARS:

_____

_____

_____

_____

_____

_____

5-10 YEARS:

_____

_____

_____

_____

_____

_____

10-15 YEARS:

_____

_____

_____

_____

_____

_____

_____

Join me on the journey toward intentional, professional motherhood - www.steadymom.com

DRAFT MISSION STATEMENT

Begin to write a draft mission statement below.

_____

_____

_____

_____

_____

DRAFT VISION STATEMENT

Begin to write a draft vision statement below.

_____

_____

_____

_____

_____

_____

_____

_____

_____

_____

_____

Join me on the journey toward intentional, professional motherhood - www.steadymom.com

Appendix B
Suggested Resources

The following titles and websites have been extremely helpful to me as I pursue intentional, professional motherhood.

Getting Organized

www.simplemom.net - Life Hacks for Home Managers

Morgenstern, Julie. *Organizing from the Inside Out: The Foolproof System for Organizing Your Home, Your Office and Your Life.* New York: Henry Holt, 2004.

Paul, Marilyn. *It's Hard to Make a Difference When You Can't Find Your Keys: The Seven-Step Path to Becoming Truly Organized.* New York: Penguin, 2003.

St. James, Elaine. *Simplify Your Life: 100 Ways to Slow Down and Enjoy the Things That Really Matter.* New York: Hyperion, 1994.

Townley Ewer, Cynthia. *Houseworks: Cut the Clutter, Speed Your Cleaning and Calm the Chaos.* New York: DK Publishing, 2006.

Retaining Enthusiasm

Bailey, Becky. *Easy to Love, Difficult to Discipline: The 7 Basic Skills for Turning Conflict into Cooperation.* New York: HarperCollins, 2001.

Campbell, Ross. *How to Really Love Your Child.* Colorado Springs, CO: David C. Cook, 2004.

Cohen, Lawrence. *Playful Parenting.* New York: Ballantine Books, 2002.

Peale, Norman Vincent. *The Power of Positive Thinking.* New York: Fireside, 2003.

Learning Together

www.amblesideonline.org/CM/toc.html - More Information about Charlotte Mason

Grant, Rae. *Crafting Fun: 101 Things to Make and Do with Kids*. New York: St. Martin's, 2008.

Holt, John. *How Children Learn*. New York: Da Capo, 1995.

Hunt, Gladys. *Honey for a Child's Heart*. Grand Rapids, MI: Zondervan, 2002.

Kuffner, Trish. *The Preschooler's Busy Book: 365 Creative Games & Activities to Occupy 3-6 Year Olds*. New York: Meadowbrook, 1998.

Trelease, Jim. *The Read-Aloud Handbook*. New York: Penguin, 2006.

Making Memories

Bailey, Becky. *I Love You Rituals*. New York: HarperCollins, 2000.

Blake Soule, Amanda. *The Creative Family: How to Encourage Imagination and Nurture Family Connections*. Boston, MA: Trumpeter, 2008.

McBride, Tracey. *Frugal Luxuries by the Seasons: Celebrate the Holidays with Elegance and Simplicity—On Any Income*. New York: Bantam, 2000.

Trainer Thompson, Jennifer. *The Joy of Family Traditions: A Season-by-Season Companion to 400 Celebrations and Activities*. Berkeley, CA: Ten Speed, 2008.

Crafting Your Mission Statement

Covey, Stephen R. *The 7 Habits of Highly Effective Families*. London: Simon & Schuster, 1999.

Jones, Laurie Beth. *The Path: Creating Your Mission Statement for Work and for Life*. New York: Hyperion, 1998.

Appendix C
Additional Sample *Steady Routines*

Use these sample routines to gather ideas for your own.

SAMPLE STEADY ROUTINE #1:
AT-HOME MOTHER WITH THREE CHILDREN

TIME/ DURATION	MOM	CHILD #1 5 Years	CHILD #2 3 Years	CHILD #3 1½ Years
6:15 AM	Up, ready for day	Sleep		
	Children up	Wake up, dress		
	Breakfast	Breakfast		
	Dishes, laundry	Free play		
(20–30 min)		Structured play: M—Sticker books T—Painting W—Baking or Legos Th—Music F—Matchbox cars Sa—Big blocks Su—Dress-up		
(30–40 min)	Cleaning/ emails	Room time		
	Snack	Snack time		

	Playtime/special activity: M—Library T—Legos or Walk W—Play-Doh Th—Park/indoor playground F—Playgroup			
(15–30 min)	Outside time or rice table			
(10–15 min)	Dance/music time			
	Lunch prep, tidy up	Video time		
	Lunch/clean-up	Lunch, free play		
	Nap prep	Free play	Free play	To bed
(30–45 min)	Preschool activities			Nap
	Children to bed, emails	Rest/book time	Nap	Nap
	Rest/read	Rest/book time	Nap	Nap
3:15 PM	Dinner prep/cleaning	Playtime	Nap	Nap
(20–30 min)	Outside play, play upstairs, or play on porch			
(10–20 min)	Read to all	Story Time		
(20–30 min)		Structured play: M—Noah's ark T—Blocks W—Dress-up T—Tent/tunnel		

(20–30 min)		F—Mr. Potato Head Sa—Legos Su—Music
	Dinner prep	Video time
	Dinner	Dinner time
(10–15 min)	Dinner clean-up	Outside play or inside dance/music
	Evening activity: M—Individual time with children (rotate) T—Drive/errands W—Coloring books/stamp art Th—Drive/errands F—Individual time with children (rotate) Sa—Dry-erase boards/chalkboards Su—Tearing/cutting & gluing	
	Rotate baths	Bath/playtime
	Bedtime routine	Ready for bed
8:00 PM	Children in bed or individual time with one child	
	Work or free time	Sleep	Sleep	Sleep

SAMPLE STEADY ROUTINE #2A:
WORKING MOM WITH ONE CHILD & IN-HOME CHILDCARE
(MON., WED., FRI. ROUTINE)

TIME/ DURATION	MOM	CHILD 3 Years	NANNY
6:30 AM	Up, prepare for day	Sleep	—
7:00 AM	Child wakes up, playtime	Wake, free play with Mom	—
7:30 AM	Check emails	Breakfast, clothes on	Arrive, child breakfast and dressed
8:00 AM	Leave for office	Read books together	
8:30 AM	Arrive at office	Structured-play time	
9:00 AM	At office	Video time	Laundry
9:30 AM	At office	Outing: M—Playgroup W—Library story time F—Tumbling class	
11:30 AM	At office	Room time	Cleaning
12:00 PM	At office	Lunch, free play	Lunch prep, clean-up
1:00 PM	At office	Naptime	Write Steady Blessings, cleaning
1:30 PM	Leave office	Sleep	Dinner prep

2:00 PM	Arrive home, rest	Sleep	Off duty
2:30 PM	Story time		—
3:00 PM	Free time		—
5:00 PM	Dinner prep	Help with dinner, play	—
5:30 PM	Dinner		—
6:00 PM	Structured play with Mom and Dad		—
6:30 PM	Art	Art	—
7:00 PM	Dinner clean-up, work	TV/video time	—
8:00 PM	Check office emails	Free play with Dad	—
8:30 PM	Give child bath	Bathtime, ready for bed	—
9:00 PM	Free	Bedtime	—

SAMPLE STEADY ROUTINE #2B:
WORKING MOM WITH ONE CHILD & IN-HOME CHILDCARE
(TUES., THURS. ROUTINE)

TIME/ DURATION	MOM	CHILD 3 Years	NANNY
6:30 AM	Sleep	Sleep	Off duty
7:00 AM	Child wakes up, playtime	Wake, free play with Mom	—
7:30 AM	Breakfast and dress child	Breakfast, clothes on	—
8:00 AM	Read books together		—
8:30 AM	Shower, dress	Video time	—
9:00 AM	Structured play		—
9:30 AM	Outing: T—Park Th—Errands		—
11:30 AM	Laundry, emails	Room time	—
12:00 PM	Lunch prep, clean-up	Lunch, free play	—
1:00 PM	Write Steady Blessings, office work	Naptime	—
1:30 PM	Dinner prep	Sleep	—
2:00 PM	Free	Sleep	—
2:30 PM	Story time		—
3:00 PM	Free time		—

5:00 PM	Dinner prep	Help with dinner, play	—
5:30 PM	Dinner		—
6:00 PM	Structured play with Mom and Dad		—
6:30 PM	Art or baking		—
7:00 PM	Dinner clean-up, work	TV/video time	—
8:00 PM	Check office emails	Free play with Dad	—
8:30 PM	Give child bath	Bathtime, ready for bed	—
9:00 PM	Free	Bedtime	—

SAMPLE STEADY ROUTINE #3:
WORKING MOM, CHILDREN IN ELEMENTARY SCHOOL

TIME/ DURATION	MOM	CHILD #1 7½ Years	CHILD #2 5 Years
6:00 AM	Wake up, ready for day	Sleep	Sleep
6:45 AM	Wake up children, help dress	Up, dress	Up, dress
	Breakfast	Breakfast	Breakfast
	Make lunches	Get backpacks ready	Get backpacks ready
7:45 AM	In van	In van	In van
8:15 AM	School drop-off	Arrive at school	Arrive at school
8:30 AM	Arrive at work	School	School
2:30 PM	Leave work	School	School
2:45 PM	School pickup	Pickup	Pickup
3:15 PM	Arrive home, snack	Home, snack	Home, snack
(2 hrs)	Play with kids, house projects	Free play at home or friend's house	
(45 min)	Make dinner	Homework/ read at dining table	Room time
	Dinner	Dinner	Dinner
	Dinner clean-up (everyone help)		

(1 hr)	TV/video time Th—Family game night		
	Help with baths	Play, bathtime	Play, bathtime
8:45 PM	Children in bed	Bedtime	Bedtime

SAMPLE STEADY ROUTINE #4:
WORKING MOM, DAD IN GRAD SCHOOL,
CHILD IN PART-TIME DAYCARE

TIME/ DURATION	MOM	CHILD 2½ Years	DAD
6:15 AM	Up, ready for day	Sleep	Sleep
7:15 AM	Leave for work	Sleep	Up, check emails
7:45 AM	Arrive at office	Wake up, free play	Shower, dress
	Office	Breakfast time	
	Office	Get child dressed, free play	
(1½ hrs)	Office	Room time/ video/ snack (MWF); outing with Dad (TTh)	School work (MWF); outing (TTh)
(30 min)	Office	Structured play (MWF); outing (TTh)	
11:30 AM	Office	Free play	Ready for class/ daycare
11:45 AM	Office	Leave home	
12:00 PM	Office	Arrive at daycare	Drop child off
12:15 PM	Office	Daycare	Arrive at school
3:30 PM	Pick up child from daycare	Pickup	Grad school

3:45 PM	Arrive home, nap prep	Home, down for nap	Grad school
	Free time	Nap	Grad school
5:00 PM	Mom/Dad time	Nap	Home; Mom/Dad time
(30 min)	Structured play		Free or school work
(15 min)	Read books		
	Computer/work time	Video	Start dinner prep
	Finish dinner prep	Video	Computer time
7:00 PM	Dinner	Dinner	Dinner
	Dinner clean-up	Free play	Dinner clean-up
(2 hrs)	M—Mom work; Dad/child outing T—Family outing W—Mom work; Dad/child play at home Th—Dad work; Mom/child outing F—Family outing Sa—Family night at home Su—Dad work; Mom/child play at home		
(30–45 min)	Child bathtime, bedtime routine		
10:15 PM	Free or work	Bedtime	Free or work

Notes

[1] Marilyn Paul, *It's Hard to Make a Difference When You Can't Find Your Keys* (New York: Penguin Group, 2003), p. 4.

[2] Andrew Clark and Orsolya Lelkes, "Let Us Pray: Religious Interactions in Life Satisfaction," *Paris-Jourdan Sciences Economiques* (PSE Working Paper No. 2009-01) (Paris, 2009); online at http://ideas.repec.org/p/pse/psecon/2009-01.html.

[3] Stephen Post, "The Power of Gratitude," *Guideposts* November 2007: pp. 78-79.

[4] Robert Emmons and Michael McCullough, "Counting Blessings Versus Burdens: An Experimental Investigation of Gratitude and Subjective Well-Being in Daily Life," *Journal of Personality and Social Psychology* Vol 84, 2003: pp. 377-389; online at http://www.psy.miami.edu/faculty/mmccullough/Gratitude_Page.htm.

[5] Henry David Thoreau, *Walden* (New York: Walter J Black, 1942), p. 348.

[6] Charlotte Mason, *School Education* (Charlotte Mason Research & Supply, 1989), pp. 170-171.

[7] Ina V. S. Mullis, John A. Dossey, Jay R. Campbell, Claudia A. Gentile, Christine Sullivan, and Andrew Lathem, *NAEP 1992 Trends in Academic Progress*, Office of Educational Research and Improvement (Washington, DC: U.S. Department of Education, June 1994).

Index

cooking, 47-48, 84
cooking chart, 48
crafting, 37, 112
creativity, 25, 37, 56, 59, 76, 91, 104
crib time, 38
cues, internal, 69-70
culture, family, 88
curiosity, 75-76, 92

D

date nights, 48
date organizer, 46
daycare, 36, 64, 85
delegate, 25
depression, 62, 68
developmental stages, 80
Dickens, Charles, 53, 75
discipline, 58, 80, 99
dishes, washing, 50
disorganization, 19, 21-23
dividers, file, 43, 106
divorce, 68
DVDs, 40, 82

E

education, 75-76, 81-82, 88,
   91-92, 111
efficiency, 19-20, 28, 50, 112, 114
Emmons, Robert, 62
emotional autopilot, 69
empathy, 69
encouragement, 55, 62, 66
energy, 22, 50, 62
enthusiasm, 13-14, 53, 55, 57-62,
   66, 68-69, 114

environment, home, 69, 91
evening routine, 31
expert, 84, 113-114

F

faith, religious, 60, 111
falling behind, 51
family culture, 88
feedings, 50
feelings, 13, 19, 24, 28, 45, 51, 57,
   69, 92
field trips, 49, 83
flexibility, 26, 36, 47, 99
flexible structure, 20-21, 27, 32, 100
follow the spark, 99
food plan, 23
formula, parenting, 64, 80
freedom, 28, 36-37, 114
free play, 31, 37
friends, 23, 36, 55, 62, 75, 78, 109

G

getting organized, 14, 17, 114
global-mindedness, 83
goals, children's, 49, 85
goals, long-term, 25, 58
grace, 113-114
gratitude, 49, 62
guilt, 21, 64, 69

H

habits, 21, 23, 27-28, 58, 64, 68,
   78-80, 91
health, 23, 30, 62, 97
heart, steady, 61

CPSIA information can be obtained
at www.ICGtesting.com
Printed in the USA
LVOW04s2239120516
488020LV00013B/156/P

9 780984 124602